Special thanks to
Jason Brooks
Dr. Matthew Eve
Takahiro Kanie
Menno Kluin
Liz Leavitt (Levine/Leavitt)
Anelle Miller
and
Anne Telford
for their professional advice and assistance.

Contents

		Archive No.	Page
Advertising			
	Takahisa Hashimoto	200bil 09.001	17
	André Paiva	200bil 09.002	18
	Jasper Wong	200bil 09.003	19
	Marloes Duyker	200bil 09.004	20
	Touko Okamura	200bil 09.005	21
	Naja Conrad-Hansen	200bil 09.006	22
	Yuhee Seo	200bil 09.006	22
	Olaf Hajek	200bil 09.007	23
	Kari Modén	200bil 09.007	23
	Olaf Hajek	200bil 09.008-009	24-25
	Geoff Harrold	200bil 09.010	26
	Joseba Elorza	200bil 09.011	27
	David von Bassewitz	200bil 09.012	28
	Danijela Dobric	200bil 09.013	29
	Kittozutto	200bil 09.014	30
	Otavio Rios	200bil 09.014	30
	Hana Akiyama	200bil 09.015	31
	Caglar Biyikoglu	200bil 09.016	32
	Carlos Araujo	200bil 09.016	32
	Anita Kunz	200bil 09.017	33
	Surachai Puthikulangkura	200bil 09.017	33
	Eduardo Tavares	200bil 09.018	34
	Dan Smith	200bil 09.019	35
	Morten Meldgaard	200bil 09.020-021	36-37
	Kako	200bil 09.021	37
	Sonya Suhariyan	200bil 09.022	38
	Stuart Briers	200bil 09.023	39
	Neryl Walker	200bil 09.023	39
	Surachai Puthikulangkura	200bil 09.024	40
	Otavio Rios	200bil 09.025	41
	Otavio Rios	200bil 09.026	42
	Mitsunari Kawamoto	200bil 09.027	43
	Andy Potts	200bil 09.028	44
	Mick Wiggins	200bil 09.029	45
	Carlos Araujo	200bil 09.030	46
	Daniel Stolle	200bil 09.031	47
	Anson Liaw	200bil 09.031	47
	Alicia Manero	200bil 09.032	48
	Pomme Chan	200bil 09.032	48

		Archive No.	Page
	Cheri Scholten	200bil 09.032	48
	Floship	200bil 09.033	49
	David von Bassewitz	200bil 09.034	50
	Michel Canetti	200bil 09.034	50
	David von Bassewitz	200bil 09.035	51
	Abigail McKenzie	200bil 09.036	52
	Marika Metsävainio	200bil 09.036	52
	Bernadette Burke	200bil 09.036	52
	Giulio Iurissevich	200bil 09.037	53
	Abigail McKenzie	200bil 09.037	53
	Julia Bereciartu	200bil 09.037	53
	Anja Kroencke	200bil 09.038	54
	Jim Cohen	200bil 09.038	54
	Showko Akane	200bil 09.039	55
	Annabelle Jasmin Verhoye	200bil 09.039	55
	Pedro Izique	200bil 09.040-041	56-57
	Anson Liaw	200bil 09.042	58
	Pedro Izique	200bil 09.043	59
	Eszter Kiskovacs	200bil 09.044	60
	2FRESH	200bil 09.045	61
	Caglar Biyikoglu	200bil 09.046	62
	Andrew Bannecker	200bil 09.046	62
	Ron Monnier	200bil 09.046	62
	Mark Joseph Deutsch	200bil 09.047	63
	Kim Rosen	200bil 09.047	63
	Brock Davis	200bil 09.047	63
	Eduardo Casassus	200bil 09.048	64
	Daniel Malecki/ExDandy	200bil 09.048	64
	Craig McGill	200bil 09.049	65
	Eduardo Tavares	200bil 09.049	65
	Brosmind Studio	200bil 09.050-051	66-67
	Justin Gabbard	200bil 09.052	68
	James O'Brien	200bil 09.052	68
	Jon Krause	200bil 09.052	68
	Justin Gabbard	200bil 09.053	69
	Frank Stockton	200bil 09.053	69
	Shane Luskie	200bil 09.054	70
	Chris Judge	200bil 09.055	71
	Eduardo Bertone	200bil 09.056	72
	Max Ellis	200bil 09.056	72

Contents

	Archive No.	Page
Edvard Scott	200bil 09.057	73
Lomp	200bil 09.057	73
Alex Zoebisch	200bil 09.058	74
Alexandre Norito Miyaki	200bil 09.059	75
Vali Petridean	200bil 09.060-061	76-77
Sunil Garud	200bil 09.062	78
Eelco van den Berg	200bil 09.062	78
Jan Feindt	200bil 09.063	79
Jan Feindt	200bil 09.064	80
Pedro Izique	200bil 09.065	81
Paul Pateman	200bil 09.065	81
Johan Potma	200bil 09.066	82
Abhishek Sawant	200bil 09.067	83
Pavel Klubnikin	200bil 09.068	84
Freddy Jana	200bil 09.068	84
Page Tsou	200bil 09.069	85
artbombers	200bil 09.070	86
Alessandro Adelio Rossi	200bil 09.071	87
Thomas Simpfendoerfer	200bil 09.072-073	88-89
Carioca	200bil 09.074-075	90-91

Books

	Archive No.	Page
Kleber Menezes	200bil 09.001-002	92-93
Daniel Malecki/ExDandy	200bil 09.003	94
Erica Dorn	200bil 09.003	94
Jamie Williams	200bil 09.004	95
David von Bassewitz	200bil 09.005-006	96-97
Cathy Gendron	200bil 09.005	96
Adrià Fruitós	200bil 09.006	97
Mattias Adolfsson	200bil 09.007	98
Craig McGill	200bil 09.007	98
David Despau	200bil 09.008	99
Patray Lui	200bil 09.009	100
Annika Sköld	200bil 09.010	101
Rahele Jomepour	200bil 09.011	102
Cheri Scholten	200bil 09.012	103
Anna Cairanti	200bil 09.013	104
Irina Troitskaya	200bil 09.013	104
Alexandra Zaharova	200bil 09.014	105
Rahele Jomepour	200bil 09.015	106

	Archive No.	Page
Catty Flores	200bil 09.015	106
Petra Kolitsch	200bil 09.016	107
Nicolas Bolasini	200bil 09.017	108
Headcase Design	200bil 09.018	109
Zsolt Vidak	200bil 09.019	110
Sergey Steblina	200bil 09.020	111
Headcase Design	200bil 09.021-022	112-113
Tina Berning	200bil 09.023-024	114-115
Kako	200bil 09.025	116

Calendars

	Archive No.	Page
Jan Feindt	200bil 09.001	117
Ana Galvan	200bil 09.002-003	118-119

Cards

	Archive No.	Page
Noper	200bil 09.001	120
Luca Laurenti	200bil 09.002	121
Lisa Kaser	200bil 09.003	122
Caglar Biyikoglu	200bil 09.003	122
Agata Janus	200bil 09.004	123
Julia Bereciartu	200bil 09.005	124
Papriko, Ink.	200bil 09.006	125
Alessandro Adelio Rossi	200bil 09.007	126
Elisa Sassi	200bil 09.008	127
Jorge Mascarenhas	200bil 09.009	128
Sean Macfarlane	200bil 09.010	129
Cathy Gendron	200bil 09.010	129
Jennifer Taylor	200bil 09.010	129
Karol Lasia	200bil 09.011-012	130-131
Caglar Biyikoglu	200bil 09.013-014	132-133
Hayato Jome	200bil 09.015	134
Caglar Biyikoglu	200bil 09.016	135
Alexander Grigorev	200bil 09.016	135
Chris Roth	200bil 09.017	136

CD Design

	Archive No.	Page
David Ho	200bil 09.001	137
Sean Mosher-Smith	200bil 09.002-003	138-139
Andres Henao	200bil 09.004	140
Vika Prokopaviciute	200bil 09.005	141

Contents

		Archive No.	Page				Archive No.	Page
	Jim Cohen	200bil 09.006	142			Jason Brooks	200bil 09.021-024	174-177
	Dan Smith	200bil 09.007	143			Lisa Billvik	200bil 09.025	178
						Ana Galvan	200bil 09.025	178
Covers						Anne Lück	200bil 09.026	179
	Hayato Jome	200bil 09.001	144			Paola Piglia	200bil 09.027-030	180-183
	James Gulliver Hancock	200bil 09.002	145			Pedro Izique	200bil 09.031	184
	Tanja Székessy	200bil 09.002	145			Edward Kinsella III	200bil 09.032	185
	Jennifer Taylor	200bil 09.003	146			Mark Timmins	200bil 09.033	186
	Mick Wiggins	200bil 09.004	147			Edel Rodriguez	200bil 09.034	187
	Graham Samuels	200bil 09.005	148			Stephen Ledwidge	200bil 09.034	187
	Steven Tabbutt	200bil 09.006	149			Jon Krause	200bil 09.034	187
	Sam Weber	200bil 09.007	150			Marco Wagner	200bil 09.035-036	188-189
	Edel Rodriguez	200bil 09.008	151			Thomas L. Fluharty	200bil 09.037	190
	Ron Monnier	200bil 09.009	152			Frank Stockton	200bil 09.038	191
	Anita Kunz	200bil 09.010	153			David von Bassewitz	200bil 09.038	191
						Jennifer Taylor	200bil 09.039-040	192-193
Magazine Editorial						David Heatley	200bil 09.041	194
	Aleksandra Knezevic	200bil 09.001-002	154-155			Marco Marella	200bil 09.042	195
	Tanja Székessy	200bil 09.003-004	156-157			Liz Lomax	200bil 09.043	196
	Josh McKible	200bil 09.005	158			Pomme Chan	200bil 09.044	197
	Alexandra Falagara	200bil 09.006	159			Jon Krause	200bil 09.045	198
	George Bates	200bil 09.005-006	158-159			Jonathan Cusick	200bil 09.046	199
	Mattias Käll	200bil 09.007	160			Mimi Leung	200bil 09.047	200
	Julia Bereciartu	200bil 09.008	161			Vadim Gannenko	200bil 09.047	200
	Scott Bakal	200bil 09.008	161			Headcase Design	200bil 09.048	201
	Viktor Melamed	200bil 09.009	162			Eduardo Bertone	200bil 09.048	201
	Elena Tsaregradskaya	200bil 09.010	163			Headcase Design	200bil 09.049-050	202-203
	Nathaniel Eckstrom	200bil 09.010	163			Jan Feindt	200bil 09.051	204
	Anita Kunz	200bil 09.011	164			Frank Stockton	200bil 09.052	205
	Noper	200bil 09.012	165			Max Ellis	200bil 09.053	206
	Kerstin Lindermeier	200bil 09.012	165			Kyle T. Webster	200bil 09.053	206
	Cathy Gendron	200bil 09.012	165			Robert Carter	200bil 09.054	207
	Yihsin Wu	200bil 09.013	166			Tymek Jezierski	200bil 09.055	208
	Juan Carlos Cabadas Reyna	200bil 09.013	166			Headcase Design	200bil 09.056	209
	Yihsin Wu	200bil 09.014	167			Mats Bergen	200bil 09.057	210
	Daniel Stolle	200bil 09.015-016	168-169			Anja Kroencke	200bil 09.058	211
	George Bates	200bil 09.017-018	170-171			Joseph Daniel Fiedler	200bil 09.059	212
	David von Bassewitz	200bil 09.019	172			Matt Murphy	200bil 09.060	213
	Jens Bonnke	200bil 09.019	172			Paul Wearing	200bil 09.061	214
	Anita Kunz	200bil 09.020	173			Stephen Ledwidge	200bil 09.062	215

	Archive No.	Page
Anja Kroencke	200bil 09.063-064	216-217
Chuanda Tan	200bil 09.065-066	218-219
Jay Taylor	200bil 09.067	220
Olaf Hajek	200bil 09.068	221

Media

	Archive No.	Page
David von Bassewitz	200bil 09.001-002	222-223
Scott Bakal	200bil 09.003	224
Martin Haussmann	200bil 09.004	225
Gili Comforty	200bil 09.005-006	226-227
Julia Ziegler	200bil 09.007	228
Sonia Hidalgo Delorme	200bil 09.008	229
PixelPastry	200bil 09.009	230
Coen Hamelink	200bil 09.010	231
Meike Andresen	200bil 09.010	231
IC4DESIGN INC./		
Hirofumi Kamigaki	200bil 09.011-012	232-233
Daniel Dociu	200bil 09.013-016	234-237
Coen Hamelink	200bil 09.017-018	238-239
Ivan Maximov	200bil 09.019	240

Posters

	Archive No.	Page
Yuji Yamada	200bil 09.001	241
Abigail McKenzie	200bil 09.002	242
Karol Guerrero	200bil 09.003	243
Irina Grabarnik	200bil 09.003	243
Edward Kinsella III	200bil 09.004	244
Kako	200bil 09.004	244
Anita Kunz	200bil 09.004	244
Norbert Horvath	200bil 09.005	245
Showko Akane	200bil 09.006	246
Sae Tachimori	200bil 09.007	247
Santiago Morilla	200bil 09.008-009	248-249
Danijela Dobric	200bil 09.010	250
Scott Bakal	200bil 09.011	251
Mitsunari Kawamoto	200bil 09.012	252
Hiromitsu Kobayashi	200bil 09.013	253
Freddy Jana	200bil 09.014	254
Mogu	200bil 09.014	254
Sonia Maria Luce	200bil 09.015	255

	Archive No.	Page
Naja Conrad-Hansen	200bil 09.015	255
Ron Monnier	200bil 09.016	256
Hayato Higasa	200bil 09.017	257
Edel Rodriguez	200bil 09.018-019	258-259
Matteo Franceschini	200bil 09.020	260
Eduardo Bertone	200bil 09.021	261
Carson Ting	200bil 09.021	261
Si Scott	200bil 09.022	262
May Ann Licudine	200bil 09.023	263
Giulio Iurissevich	200bil 09.024	264
Tessa Benders	200bil 09.024	264
Johnny Cheuk	200bil 09.024	264
Olaf Hajek	200bil 09.025	265
Mimi Leung	200bil 09.026	266
sLip	200bil 09.027	267
Anja Nolte	200bil 09.027	267
Johanna Velasco	200bil 09.027	267
Caroline Stirling	200bil 09.028	268
Thomas L. Fluharty	200bil 09.029	269
Stephane Goddard	200bil 09.030	270
Juan Patino	200bil 09.031	271
Andrew Bannecker	200bil 09.031	271
Mick Wiggins	200bil 09.032	272
Neryl Walker	200bil 09.033	273

Products

	Archive No.	Page
Jeff Nishinaka	200bil 09.001	274
Ilya Kolesnikov	200bil 09.002	275
Jasper Wong	200bil 09.003	276
Noumeda Carbone	200bil 09.004	277
Jan Feindt	200bil 09.005	278
Annabelle Jasmin Verhoye	200bil 09.006	279
Alexandre Norito Miyaki	200bil 09.007	280
Tatiana Arocha	200bil 09.008	281

	Page
Index A-M	3, 288
Index M-Z	4, 290
Credits	10
Selection Criteria	11
Interview	12-16
Index to Illustrators	282-287

Lürzer's **Special** **ARCHIVE**

Lürzer's Archive Special
200 Best Illustrators worldwide 09/10
(ISSN 1816-9589)

Publisher & Editor: Walter Lürzer **Editor-in-chief:** Michael Weinzettl **Production Manager:** Eva Henle **Editorial Assistants:** Victoria Morgan, Alexandra A. Nementh, Stephanie Sutanto, Stephanie Teresa Sutter **Layout:** Gabi Kratzer **Marketing & Sales Manager:** Sandra Lehnst **Sales Representatives:** Kate Brown, Claudia Coffman, Diana Dragomir, Sheila King, Carina Wicke

Administration/Editorial Office: Lürzer GmbH, Keinergasse 29, 1030 Vienna, Austria, phone: (43) 1 715 24 24, office@luerzers archive.com, submission@luerzersarchive.com

Printers: BGR Druck-Service GmbH, Ferdinand-Porsche-Straße 51, 60386 Frankfurt am Main, Germany, phone: (49) 69 94 34 25-0 fax: (49) 69 94 34 25-30 **Pre-Press:** DMSmedia, Peregrinstraße 8, 5020 Salzburg, Austria, phone: (43) 662 84 41 95, fax: (43) 662 84 41 95-95, office@dmsmedia.at

Submission of material to Lürzer's Archive constitutes representation that the submitter has the authority to grant and grants Lürzer's Archive the right and permission to reproduce, edit and comment editorially on all or any part of the submission in Lürzer's Archive's editorial section. All such reproductions are free of charge to the submitter. Lürzer's Archive assumes no responsibility to return unsolicited material, and reserves the right to accept or reject any advertising material for any reason.

Distributors:
Argentina: *La Paragrafica*, tool@paragrafica. com.ar **Australia:** *Selectair Distribution Services*, sales@selectair.com.au **Brazil:** *Livraria Freebook Ltda.*, manuel@freebook. com.br; *Casa Ono Com. e Imp. Ltda.*, casaono@uol.com.br; *Open Books*, romeu @openbooks. com.br **Bulgaria:** *Milen Marchev*, archive@milenmarchev.com **Canada:** *Keng Seng Enterprises Inc.*, canada@ kengseng.com **China:** *Beijing Designers-books, importo1@designerbooks.com.cn* **Colombia:** *Diseño Y Tecnica*, distecnica @hotmail. com; *Foto Colombia*, stamayo @fotocolombia. com **Costa Rica:** *BAUM S.A.*, baumsa@racsa.co.cr **Czech Republik:** *ADC Czech Republic*, info@adc-czech.cz **Denmark:** *Tegnecenter*, info@tegnecenter. dk **Dominican Republic:** *Portfolio Group*, wendolyn@portfoliodr.com **Finland:** *Suomalainen Kirjakauppa*, tom.nordstrom @suomalainenkk.fi **France:** *Lürzer's Archive*, (Interlocuteur Français), office@ luerzersarchive.com **Germany:** *IPS Datenservice GmbH*, abo-archiv@ips-d.de **Ghana:** *Chini Productions Ltd.*, archive @ chiniproductions.com **Greece:** *Studio Bookshop*, office@studiobookshop.com **Hong Kong:** *Keng Seng Trading & Co. Ltd.*, lawrence@kengseng.com **Hungary:** *Librotrade Kft.*, periodicals@librotrade.hu **India:** *ISBD*, sbds@bol.net.in **Indonesia:** *Basheer Graphic Books*, abdul @basheergraphic. com **Italy:** *Ellesette*, ellesette@ellesette. com; *RED*, info@redonline.it **Japan:** *DIP*, erol@dip-inc.com **Korea:** *Yi Sam Sa*, yss23k@kornet.net **Latvia:** *Valters un Rapa*, santa@valtersunrapa.lv **Malaysia:** *The Other Bookstore*, hajaotherbookstore@ yahoo.com **Moldavia:** *Mesageria D&D*, mesageriadd@gmail.com **Mexico:** *Rolando de la Piedra*, hosrpb@prodigy.net.mx **Netherlands/Belgium:** *Bruil & Van de Staaij*, info@bruil.info **New Zealand:** *Mercury Subs. Ltd.*, stuart@mercurysubs.co.nz **Nigeria:** *Chini Productions*, archive@chini productions.com **Norway:** *Luth & Co/ Font Shop*, info@luth.no **Panama:** *Latin Magazine Group*, csmith@publicist.com **Peru:** *Libreria Mediatica*, mediatica@ ec-red.com **Poland:** *VFP Communications*, kehrt@media.com.pl **Portugal:** *Marka Lda.*, apoio.clientes@marka.pt; *Tema Lda.*, belmiro@mail.telepac.pt **Romania:** *Prior Books*, ion.arzoiu@prior.ro **Russia:** *Index-Market*, info@indexmarket.ru **Singapore:** *Basheer Graphic Books*, abdul@basheer graphic.com; *Page One*, pageone@ singnet.com.sg **Slovakia:** *Archive F.K.*, predplatne@predplatne.net **Slovenia/Albania/Bosnia & Herzegovina/Croatia/Macedonia/Serbia & Montenegro:** *New Moments D.O.O.*, ideas@newmoment.si **South Africa:** *Biblioteq*, rotem_is@mac.com; *International Subscription Services*, isscc@ icon.co.za **Spain:** *Comercial Atheneum S.A.*, suscri.bcn @atheneum.com; *Promotora De Prensa*, evelazquez@promopress.es **Sri Lanka:** *Leo Burnett Solutions Inc.*, swarna_goonetillke @leoburnett.lk **Sweden:** *Svenska Interpress*, info@interpress.se **Taiwan:** *Far Go Chen Co. Ltd.*, fargo899@ms35.hinet.net **Thailand:** *B2S Co. Ltd.*, YiSorrapong@ b2s.co.th **Turkey:** *Alternatif*, alternatif@ grafikkitaplari.com; *Evrensel*, evrensely @superonline.com **Ukraine:** *DAN*, olga@ ceo.com.ua; *All-Ukrainian Advertising Coalition*, mial@adcoalition.org.ua **United Arab Emirates/Bahrein/Kuwait/Oman/Saudi Arabia/Qatar:** *MBR Bookshop LLC*, asoni@emi rates.net.ae **United Kingdom/Ireland:** *Central Books*, sasha@centralbooks.com; *Timscris*, kb@luerzersarchive.com **Uruguay:** *Graffiti S.R.L.*, graffiti@fastlink.com.uy **United States:** *Lürzer's Archive Inc.*, custsvc_ archive @fulcoinc.com **Venezuela:** *April Itriago*, april.itriago@gmail.com **All other countries:** *IPS*, Meckenheim, Germany, (English speaking), sub-archive@ips-d.de

How to use your Archive:
Guide to symbols: ⌂: Advertising Agency ▭▸: Art Director ▭▸: Copywriter ▣: Photographer ♈: Client ♈: Modelmaker ♈: Illustrator Ⓐ: Typographer ♈: Digital Artist ▭: Production Company ▮: Director

All editorial material reproduced in Lürzer's Archive Special are categorized by product, e.g. "Cards." Product groups are shown alphabetically. Every editorial page is cross-referenced with an Archive number, the first two digits indicating the year in which the special was published, and the second three digits being continuous page numbers for that particular product group. For example, 200bil 09.001 under "Cards" indicates the Volume published in 2009, and page 1 of that product group.

Cover page:
♈: Edel Rodriguez ♈: Time

The facts behind the figures

For this, the third volume in our biennial "200 Best Illustrators" series, we have again managed to assemble an excellent crop of illustrators that mixes some established names with a wealth of exciting new talents. In fact, of the 200 illustrators showcased in 09/10, only 48 appeared in one of the previous two volumes. On the pages that follow, you will, in other words, have a chance to discover the work of 152 artists not previously seen in our Illustrators series.

The selection criteria for "200 Best Illustrators" are the same as those applying to all of our "200 Best" volumes:

1) Each illustrator invited to submit work for publication in the book had to be nominated by an art director working for an ad agency or by a publishing house. This is how the 152 illustrators new to this series – and on show in this issue – got their first chance to be in the volume, and to be among what turned out to be a record-breaking total of 4,716 submissions from 44 countries.

2) Where not recommended by a professional from advertising or magazine publishing, an illustrator's work must have previously appeared in an Archive publication. This was the route taken by the 48 illustrators that had already been featured in the first or second volume of 200 Best Illustrators. (Just for the record: only ten illustrators whose work appears in this issue have held down a place in all three editions.)

3) Only illustrations published during the past 18 months were eligible. Whether this work was published as part of an advertising campaign, a magazine editorial, or in any other form (including self-promotional purposes), was of secondary importance. Of all the submissions, a final 502 illustrations made it into the book by successfully negotiating the critical scrutiny of no less than two juries: the preselection jury which – once again – consisted of Dr. Matthew Eve, post-doctoral research fellow in the Typography and Graphic Communications Dept. at the University of Reading, freelance writer and book illustrator, and Michael Weinzettl, Editor-in-chief of Lürzer's Archive. Their deliberations acted as pre-filter for the main jury, which was made up of:

- Jason Brooks, one of the world's top illustrators (for an interview with Jason, please turn to the following page)
- Takahiro Kanie, illustrator and President of the Japanese Society of Illustrators
- Menno Kluin, one-time Lürzer's Archive Student of the Year and now a successful art director who won several Cannes Lions for his former agency Saatchi & Saatchi, New York, and is currently with Y & R, New York
- Liz Leavitt of New York-based artists' agency Levine/Leavitt
- Anelle Miller, Executive Director of the Society of Illustrators, New York
- Anne Telford, Editor-at-large of Communication Arts magazine

We should like to take this opportunity to express our sincerest appreciation to the jurors for the invaluable discernment they brought to their task, and for their significant input to the making of this volume.

Below is a chart providing an at-a-glance overview of the top 15 countries featured, together with comparative figures for the last two issues. The most noticeable change from 07/08 is the decline in featured illustrators from the US as well as from Germany, which fell by 18 – from 63 to 45 – and by 15 – from 30 to 15 – respectively. Whether this drop was due to the economic crisis, which has, of course, also affected illustrators – though probably to a lesser degree than ad photographers – remains debatable. On the other hand, the sharpest increase in work featured can be seen in the case of Japan, which had six illustrators in the previous issue and now racks up an impressive total of 15, while Russia went from a single illustrator in Vol. 07/08 to a total of nine, i.e. up by eight – the same increase as that posted by Sweden, which is now represented by ten illustrators.

As well as being sold through the customary book trade channels, a total of 30,000 copies of 200 Best Illustrators worldwide 09/10 will be circulated to art buyers throughout the world by our distributors based in no less than 35 different countries. We shall also be mailing out 15 copies on behalf of each illustrator featured in 200 Best Illustrators worldwide, and each will also be represented by a Personal Showcase at www.luerzersarchive.com, enabling them to upload 12 selected images of their own best work to a website boasting 10 million hits and 100,000 visitors per month.

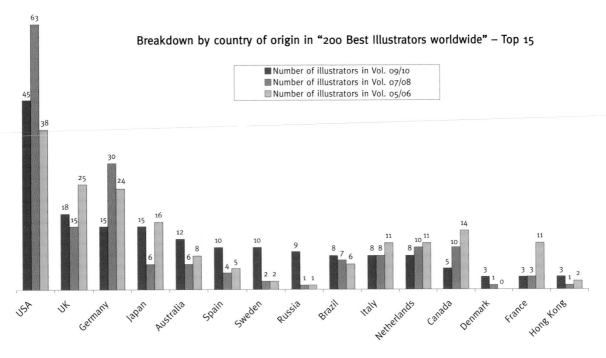

Breakdown by country of origin in "200 Best Illustrators worldwide" – Top 15

- Number of illustrators in Vol. 09/10
- Number of illustrators in Vol. 07/08
- Number of illustrators in Vol. 05/06

I have lots of ideas and dreams in reserve.

One of today's best-known illustrators, Jason Brooks first came to prominence with the wave of artists spearheading the renaissance of the illustration medium in the 1990s. His work is instantly recognizable on account of its glamorous style, and he holds a unique position in the high-end illustration market, most notably in the field of fashion-related commissions. His impressive client list includes names as prestigious as Vogue, Elle, Guerlain, Nike, Smart, Orange, Fabergé, Condé Nast Traveler, Carlsberg, Cosmopolitan, Veuve Clicquot, British Airways, and many more. Jason Brooks was kind and generous enough to serve as one of the judges for the selection of work presented in this volume. Find out more about Jason's views on illustration, and his long and illustrious career, in the following interview with Michael Weinzettl.

L.A.: I read you've been an illustrator since your early teens. Can you tell us how that came about?

Jason Brooks: Like many teenagers, I had a slightly misguided entrepreneurial spirit and I used to send illustrations to windsurfing companies and magazines, my passion at that age, in the hope that they would write back to me and, perhaps, send me stickers and that kind of thing. Sometimes, the magazines would publish little drawings I sent them and, at about 13, my first big job arrived. It was a commission to illustrate the cover of a sail brochure and

Jason Brooks   Photo: Ben Read

I remember being terribly excited when, in the post, a beautiful windsurfing sail in colors and a design that I had chosen arrived. Before then, I had been drawing avidly almost from the moment I could hold a pencil. At five or six, my school would sometimes ask me to illustrate the covers of programmes for school events, and my dad would sometimes say things like, "Can you draw me an iceberg falling into a volcano?" on his way to work, which I would then delight in having ready when he got back. As a child, I think I learned early that this activity that I loved so much also got a positive and pleasurable response from others (which probably encouraged me to do it more).

L.A.: So how did your career continue? You went to St Martins, didn't you? What was that like?

Jason Brooks: Well, after a year's foundation course in Brighton I got a place at St Martins in Covent Garden, London, in my early 20s, which was a fantastic experience during a wonderful era for the college. Sadly, the building is no longer a college, just another clothes store, but at that time it was a building full to the brim with energy and ideas. Every day felt like walking into a big party full of interesting and talented young people and colorful characters. The fashion students, as you can imagine, would often turn up in outrageous outfits reflecting their current work – floor-length coats covered in soft toys, gigantic fluoro trainers, catsuits printed with fluffy clouds, and paint-spattered ballgowns. There also existed a real ethos of hard work and a kind of healthy competition where ideas and influences were freely exchanged. While I was at St Martins, I became passionate about travel and would save up each term to take off to different parts of the world with my girlfriend during the holidays. We traveled all over Europe, Mexico, New York, Central America, and I would fill up old sketchbooks I bought in local shops and take photographs. I think all of those images and experiences provided me with a lot of material to call on when I had to draw different things, people and places later on.

L.A.: What got you interested in fashion illustration?

Jason Brooks: I've always loved drawing people and what they wear, and when I look back I can trace an interest in clothes as well as what people look like, physically, in my work. At St Martins, I won a fashion illustration

Two Martini ads illustrated by Jason Brooks.

Two collages for Elle magazine from the mid-1990s.

Jason Brooks: I liked clean uncorrected lines on paper, to which I added color with collage, paint, magic marker, nail-polish, soluble crayon – anything I could find that made an interesting mark. If I was doing what I called re-portage illustration in ink, I would make little notes on the colors of things and add in watercolor later, but I experimented with all sorts of media and styles. Another thing I often wanted to achieve was flat color, which was actually quite difficult using traditional media, and led to various experimental phases with gouache and collage.

L.A.: You were one of the very first illustrators to embrace computer technology for your work? How come?

Jason Brooks: I made my first computer images in the very late 80s while still living at home with my parents, using a very primitive color drawing program called Archimedes on a computer we had in the house. The technology obviously evolved amazingly through the 90s, and that eventually provided the means of combining line-drawing with flat color that I had been striving for. Some of my early Vogue illustrations were also created on a computer in around 1991, so, having grown up using computers to make images, I have always seen them as just another tool to reach for. People still talk about "computer art" with a certain stigma attached, as if the machine does everything for you, but they wouldn't call painting "brush art" and expect to pick up a brush and paint the Mona Lisa. The creativity of the artist is still the important ingredient, so who knows what I might be using to make images in ten years' time.

L.A.: You become known for a very specific type of illustration early on in your career. Has this highly recognizable style at times been a burden?

Jason Brooks: Well, I am very grateful for the success I've had but I did notice that, after a certain point in my career, I became permanently very busy with jobs and projects lined up one after another, and no real gaps in between. This has meant that, in a strange way, I have been led by commercial forces and what the market demanded, rather than purely by my own creative impulses. There hasn't always been time yet to experiment and express myself in other disciplines but my work has evolved and is evolving so, hopefully, as my life pans out I will have a chance to express myself further in other styles and media. I have lots of ideas and

competition run by British Vogue, which began a long series of my illustrations appearing in the magazine. I entered the competition quite instinctively without really thinking about it, just before going off to Mexico for the summer, so when I got back and I had won this rather grand-sounding award, "The Cecil Beaton Award for Fashion Illustration," I suddenly realized this was perhaps something I could do. Next, I went off to the Royal College of Art and was based for the next few years on All Saints Road, just next to Portobello market, which was really a visual feast for someone like me. I also began drawing regularly at fashion shows around this time in London, New York and Paris, reporting for newspapers and fashion magazines at shows ranging from the most avant-garde underground ones in ware-

houses, where girls wore dresses made of clingfilm, to the heights of Paris couture excess and glamorousness, so in a way I created my own fashion course after college and learned about how the industry works from many different sides. I also created club flyers around this time for "Pushca," who threw large-scale very lavish parties around London during the 90s, and also worked freelance for different ad agencies and record companies. Photography in the early to mid-nineties was very much the dominant art form and was going through a boom of its own, coupled with difficult economic times, so it was hard to find work but, gradually, illustration began to become more and more popular.

L.A.: What was your style like at the time? I assume this was before computers?

dreams in reserve, and I feel inspired to do lots of different things, so it's not something that I worry about.

L.A.: Have there, over the course of your career, been attempts to break away from your specific style, and how did people react to this?

Jason Brooks: The opportunity to break away from my particular style hasn't arrived very often. And when it has, it's difficult finding time to really develop alternative kinds of work. I love having a chance to work in different styles sometimes, and I've had a good reaction to my looser drawings, which are also much, much quicker to do, so that is one area I would like to practice and develop as I also really enjoy that.

L.A.: How would you say your style has evolved since you first became well-known?

Jason Brooks: I think my style has become more polished and realistic over the years, and I pay more attention to small details, because my illustrations can be used at many different scales, from the size of a CD cover up to billboard size. This has meant I pay attention now to small things like eyelashes or light reflecting on a fingernail whereas, before, I could get away with something a bit more expressive and sketchy. Some of my first regularly published illustrations in fashion magazines were mainly in a very time-consuming collage style, which had very few drawn lines at all. Then, when I switched completely to drawings scanned into computers, I kept a strong black line from the original drawing and

dropped in colors with the Paintbucket tool. Gradually, I have been more influenced by photography and I like making things have a more real appearance with three-dimensional volume and space, although they are still obviously drawings and largely from imagination. More recently, I'm returning to drawings that look like drawings again.

L.A.: You're also one of the most copied illustrators in the world. There are thousands of copycats doing work that resembles yours. How do you feel about that? Is imitation the "sincerest form of flattery"?

Jason Brooks: It is amazing, really, how my work seems to have inspired so many people to try and copy it. One of my friends, the great illustrator David Downton, said to me that I had created a monster with my style because it has been copied so widely, and some of the results, I have to say, are frightening. Overall, I am flattered and I'm quite relaxed about it, because if my work has inspired other people to draw and make images, that is something to be proud of. The downside is when my own real work is confused with bad copies, and people think I have done something that is pretty awful. Another downside is obviously the legal issue, and each year I have to take action against pirates somewhere who are infringing my copyright, which I have to take a lot more seriously.

L.A.: Have you found differences in working for editorial purposes compared to working for advertising clients? Is there, in other words, a difference be-

Fashion drawing from the 1990s.

tween working for, say, Vogue and for an ad agency handling Carlsberg beer?

Jason Brooks: Projects generally become more intense as the budget goes up but I think taking care over anything that leaves my studio is very important, no matter who it is for. The aim for me as an illustrator is that the person commissioning the illustrations is as happy as possible with the end product, and that it also performs the function it is meant to do out in the world. This is a challenge but it is what makes it so interesting for me too.

L.A.: What, for you, is the ideal collaboration with an art director?

Jason Brooks: An ideal collaboration starts with being on the same wavelength, and being enthusiastic about a project or idea together; it's when a conversation leads to the spark of a new direction that we hadn't seen before talking. I also like people who can be decisive and have a clear idea of what they want, or know it when they see it. Working with others is also one of the most fun things about being an illustrator, especially when it improves and enhances the end result.

L.A.: Have you had many of that kind in your career? Did any stand out?

Jason Brooks: I am lucky to have worked with lots of really nice people over the years, and I enjoy the collaborative process. The first art director I worked for at Vogue, Paul Eustace, does stand out as a great influence near the beginning of my career. He was happy with me changing style to suit the brief and really experimenting, and there were also rarely any changes because he respected my creative decisions.

Illustration for a Finlandia Vodka ad from the late 1990s.

Antigua Guatemala Sketchbook 1990

Jason Brooks

...ooks, compiled during his 1990 trips to Guate-

influences and heroes as I grew up and started out. The first illustrators I remember from my childhood were Hergé, Laurent de Brunhoff, Maurice Sendak, Tomi Ungerer, Steinberg, Raymond Briggs, Dulac, Ardizzone ... lots of the great illustrators of children's books captured my imagination and inspired me as a child. I loved Tintin books and vintage American comics in particular from four or five onwards and then, when I was six, we had a family holiday to Tuscany where I saw, for the first time, Renaissance painting and sculpture, which was a very formative experience and really opened my eyes to a new world. Later, in my teens, I loved il-

lustrators like Zoltan and Pierre Le-Tan and the great Antonio but, by then, I was also fascinated by Picasso, Degas, Matisse, Schiele, Warhol's drawings, Rodin and Renaissance artists like Botticelli, Leonardo, and Michelangelo. I also have a real love of English abstract art from the mid-20th century, particularly Ben Nicholson, Victor Pasmore, and Barbara Hepworth's sculptures. There's something very calming and Zen-like about their work, and I love how it seems to evoke nature and the beach, things also close to my heart.

L.A.: Where do you see the borderline between illustration and art? Do the two frequently overlap?

Jason Brooks: I believe all the arts are very much interconnected and, often, these boundaries and labels are to do with the intention behind a piece of work and the commercial markets they occupy. Some artists, like Paola Rego or Peter Doig, for example, could be brilliant illustrators but their work has a different, more personal message and operates in a completely different way. On the flipside, some illustrators and photographers produce work that could just as easily be fine art but it fulfills a different purpose, so it comes down to the intention behind the creativity. I think the high and low art boundaries are interesting but the "Emperor's New Clothes" phenomenon only applies to forms of art that don't have a clear function other than to be a commodity, so famous fine artists can sometimes get away with producing less good art that still sells. Being an illustrator is actually very technically demanding because there is nowhere to hide. And a picture can't be bolstered or given false meaning by long and complicated supporting text.

L.A.: What is some of your work you are proudest of?

Jason Brooks: It would have to be the travel sketchbooks made in my twenties – if there was a fire, I would save them after my family, so I suppose they must be the things I am most proud of. To be honest, I'm not someone who looks back and feels pride; I always feel a slight dissatisfaction with everything I have done before and hope my next piece of work will be better.

L.A.: What, to you, are some of the most important differences between photography and illustration?

Jason Brooks: Photography essentially captures a moment in time and is a mechanical process that gathers light from the surfaces in front of the photogra-

A 2009 illustration for the Swiss Lottery.

pher and freezes that gathered information into an image. Today, that image can then be manipulated but it is a medium that springs in quite a direct way from reality. I think illustration springs in a more direct way purely from imagination, rather than from what is presented in front of us. Who is to say which is more real.

L.A.: Would you say that illustration is a better medium, in a commercial context, to target women rather than men?

Jason Brooks: Not really. There are different kinds of illustration for all different purposes, and I find just as many men as women seem to enjoy illustration. Perhaps men and women like different styles of illustration but I believe illustration can be used commercially to appeal to either.

L.A.: What advice would you give a young illustrator who has just started out?

Jason Brooks: I would say, travel and see as much of the world as you can. This will give you a library of images to use in your work later when it might not be so easy to get away. Draw and take photos as much as you can to enhance and help capture all those memories. And try to find your own style through practicing drawing from life.

L.A.: What do you think are some of the current illustration trends, also as perceived by you when judging this book?

Jason Brooks: There is still a decorative trend going on, another trend for using photography as a starting point.

L.A.: If you close your eyes and think of the image that struck you most in the past weeks, which one would that be? Is it an illustration or a photographic image?

Jason Brooks: It would be a moving image. I saw some super slow-motion high-definition film shot by Bali Strickland from underwater inside a Pacific breaking wave, which was astonishing. It showed tiny vortices of water that followed the wave crest underwater and gave a real sense of the feeling of being inside a tubing wave. I find nature incredibly inspiring and often use the sea in my work, so it was striking to see something natural in a new way through the latest technology.

L.A.: How do you feed your imagination? Where do you get your inspiration?

Jason Brooks: Going to galleries, looking at architectural books, fashion photography, cinema and interior design – all inspire me, as well as people I know and real life around me. I might notice my wife putting her shoes on in a certain way, or make a mental note of light reflecting in a window as a silhouette passes by on the street. I live between Brighton by the sea and Kent in the English countryside but also spend a lot of time in London, so I discover varied inspiration in all of those places.

L.A.: You were one of the illustrators that rang in the big renaissance of illustration in the 90s. Has illustration gone from strength to strength since then, or has the interest waned? Where are we now at this moment in time?

Jason Brooks: The initial boom of the 90s, which seemed focused on a small number of us, has spread out and, now, illustration seems to be used much more widely, with more great illustrators around than ever. When I first left college, I almost wished it was the 1950s because I imagined all the great work I would be doing and there

seemed no demand for illustration. That changed with the advent of new ways of making images and a reinvention of traditional ways of working. Now, screen-based images are ubiquitous, and we are all used to seeing a myriad of images every day that have been created in pixels. It is up to us to take illustration forward and keep it exciting by innovating and finding new ways of doing things. I think the wonderful work in this book demonstrates that illustration is very much alive, and if we can make images that are vibrant, powerful or different, people will always be interested.

L.A.: How has the crisis affected the medium of illustration?

Jason Brooks: The economic problems the world is tackling at the moment have made it harder for illustrators to secure new work, payments are taking longer to arrive, and budgets have shrunk. On a more positive note, I have also noticed the medium holding its own as some companies turn to illustration as a less expensive option to photography that can make their company or product stand out and communicate in a competitive market. Some people may see illustration as a less safe option to photography but, in a recession, playing safe doesn't always work. Diversity in visual communication isn't going to go away, and a recession doesn't have to create a colorless landscape around us. On the contrary: people may, in more difficult times, need more than ever the joy, imagination and escapism that illustrations like those in this book can provide, so there is a lot to be optimistic about.

☺: Takahisa Hashimoto ♙: Ogilvy & Mather, Tokyo ♡: Tokyo-Yoga.com

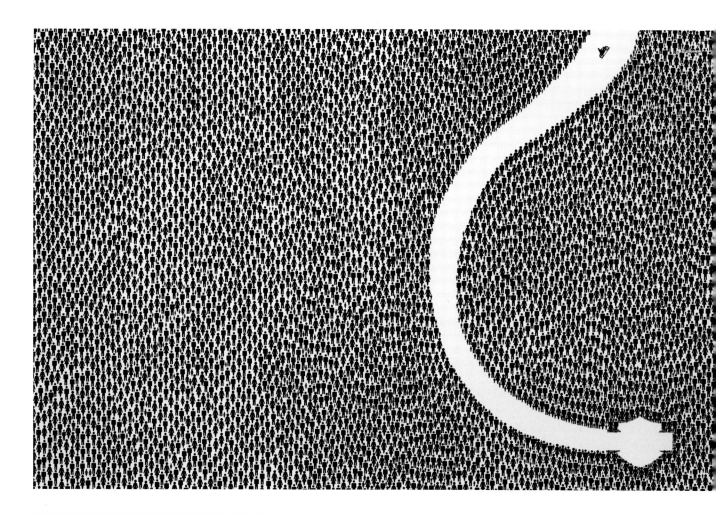

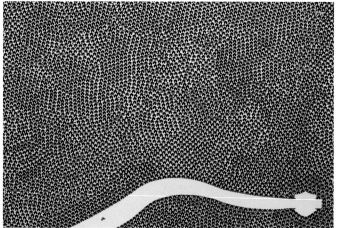

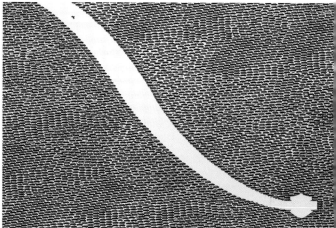

☺: André Paiva ⌂: MatosGrey, São Paulo ♕: Harley-Davidson

Ⓒ: Jasper Wong Ⓦ: Self-promotion

☺: Marloes Duyker ♔: Fortis Bank

☺: Marloes Duyker ♔: Amsterdam International Fashion Week

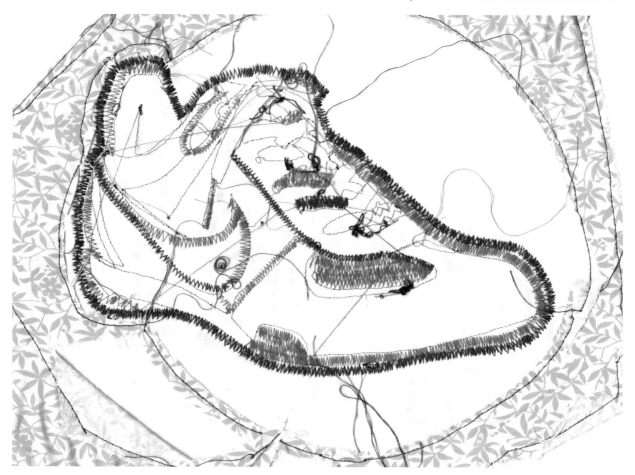

☺: Marloes Duyker ♔: Self-promotion

♡: Touko Okamura ▭: Hiroyasu Numano ♛: CROSSCO Co., Ltd.

Ⓒ: Naja Conrad-Hansen 👑: Zitty Berlin

Ⓒ: Naja Conrad-Hansen 👑: Meannorth

Ⓒ: Yuhee Seo 👑: Self-promotion

⊙: Olaf Hajek ♛: Weberbank

⊙: Kari Modén ♛: J&B Whisky

⚙: Olaf Hajek 👑: Design Hotels

☉: Olaf Hajek ♡: Charlotte Ehinger-Schwarz

⌚: Geoff Harrold ♛: Self-promotion

☻: Joseba Elorza ♔: MunduariMundo

☺: David von Bassewitz ♔: Jitter-Magazine Contest

©: Danijela Dobric ♡: Self-promotion

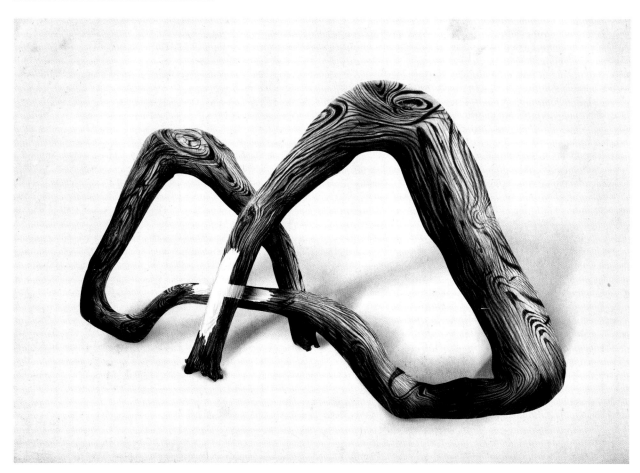

☺: Kittozutto ♔: Accept & Proceed

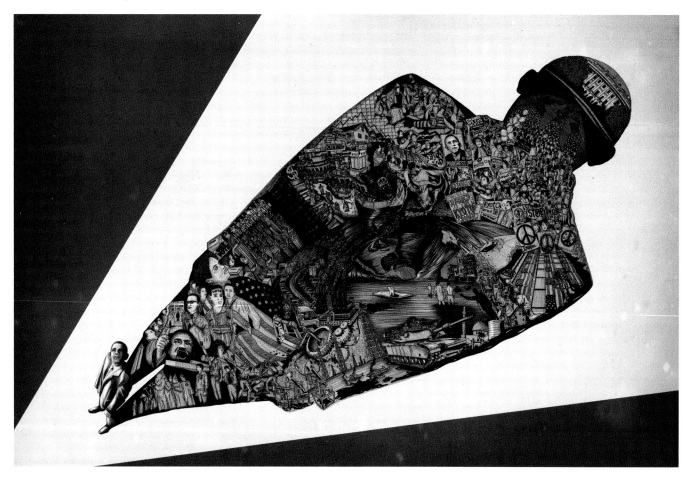

☺: Otavio Rios ♠: Africa, São Paulo ☞: Paulo Junger ♔: Folha de São Paulo

⏱: Hana Akiyama 👑: Shinbiyo Shuppan

⏱: Hana Akiyama 👑: Kenji Sawada

☺: Caglar Biyikoglu ♛: Self-promotion

☺: Carlos Araujo ♛: Self-promotion

Ⓒ: Anita Kunz ♕: Gallery Hugo

Ⓒ: Surachai Puthikulangkura ♕: WWF

⏱: Eduardo Tavares ⌂: Exclam, Curitiba, Brazil ▭: Eduardo Tavares ♔: Ponto de Fuga Illustrations

☺: Dan Smith ⚑: Engine Creative, Northampton ♛: Renaissance

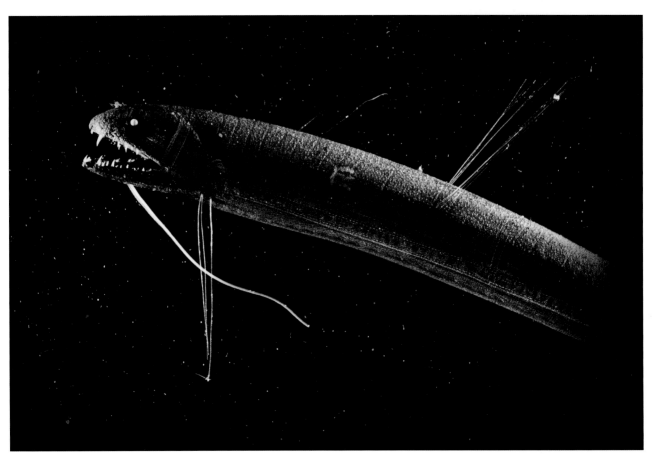

☺: Morten Meldgaard 🖫: Rasmus Petersen, Lasse Hinke ♔: Quiksilver

☺: Kako ♇: AlmapBBDO, São Paulo 🖫: Suzana Haddad ♔: Companhia das Letras

⊘: Sonya Suhariyan ♈: Illustration Ltd.

⏱: Stuart Briers ✏: Hazel Brown 👑: Radio Times

⏱: Neryl Walker 👑: Self-promotion

☺: Surachai Puthikulangkura ⌒: Leo Burnett & Arc Worldwide, Bangkok ⌯: Piti Pongrakananon ♔: Fire Engine Imperial

☻: Otavio Rios ☖: Projeto Luz

☻: Otavio Rios ♛: Brasil no Clima

⏱: Mitsunari Kawamoto 👑: Recruit

⌚: Andy Potts ⌂: Saatchi & Saatchi, New York
▭: Marcie Heffron ♕: I Love New York tourist board

⌚: Andy Potts ⌂: Bunker ▭: Francesco Ceccarelli ♕: Carraro

○: Mick Wiggins ♡: Badger Brewery

☾: Carlos Araujo ♔: Brazilian Prêmio Colunistas

☾: Carlos Araujo ♔: Self-promotion

☺: Daniel Stolle ♛: Self-promotion

☺: Anson Liaw ♛: Self-promotion

♔: Alicia Manero ♔: Abducida

♔: Pomme Chan ▭: Dawn Squance ♔: Marc Jacobs

♔: Cheri Scholten ♔: Self-promotion

☺: Floship ♔: Self-promotion

©: David von Bassewitz ♕: Specler Film Art

©: Michel Canetti ♕: Becquet

©: David von Bassewitz ♕: HBV HörBild Verlag

⊘: Abigail McKenzie ♔: Self-promotion

⊘: Marika Metsävainio ♔: Self-promotion

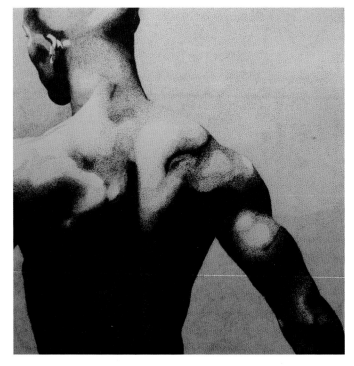

⊘: Bernadette Burke ♔: Self-promotion

☺: Giulio Iurissevich ♕: Self-promotion

☺: Abigail McKenzie ♕: Self-promotion

☺: Julia Bereciartu ♕: Self-promotion

⏱: Anja Kroencke ♛: Mitsukoshi

⏱: Jim Cohen ♛: Hawthorn Dairy

☺: Showko Akane ♛: Renaissance Academy

☺: Annabelle Jasmin Verhoye ♛: Opera Gallery

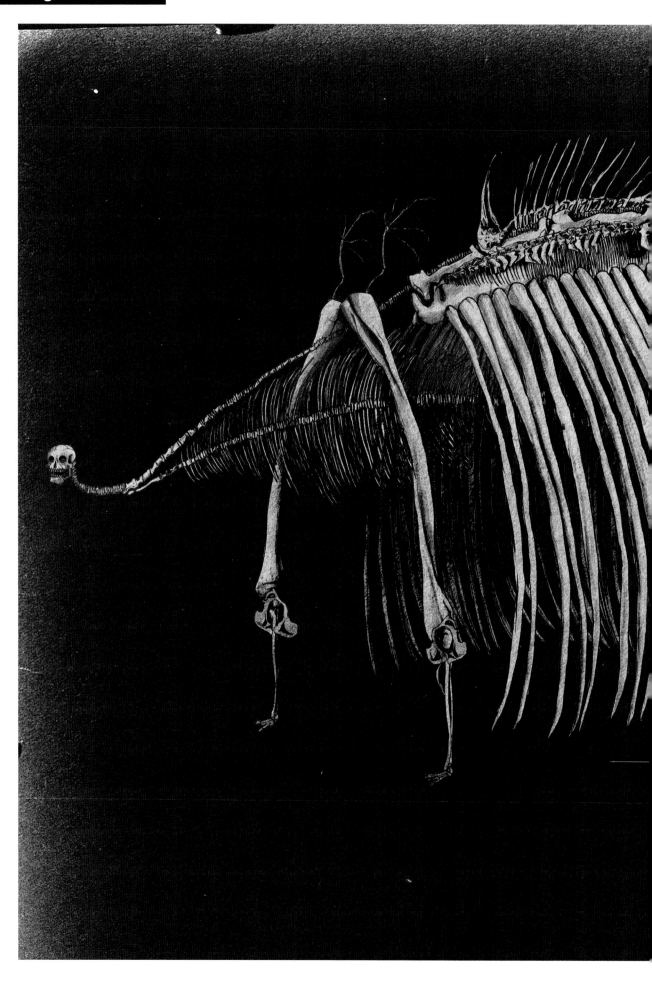

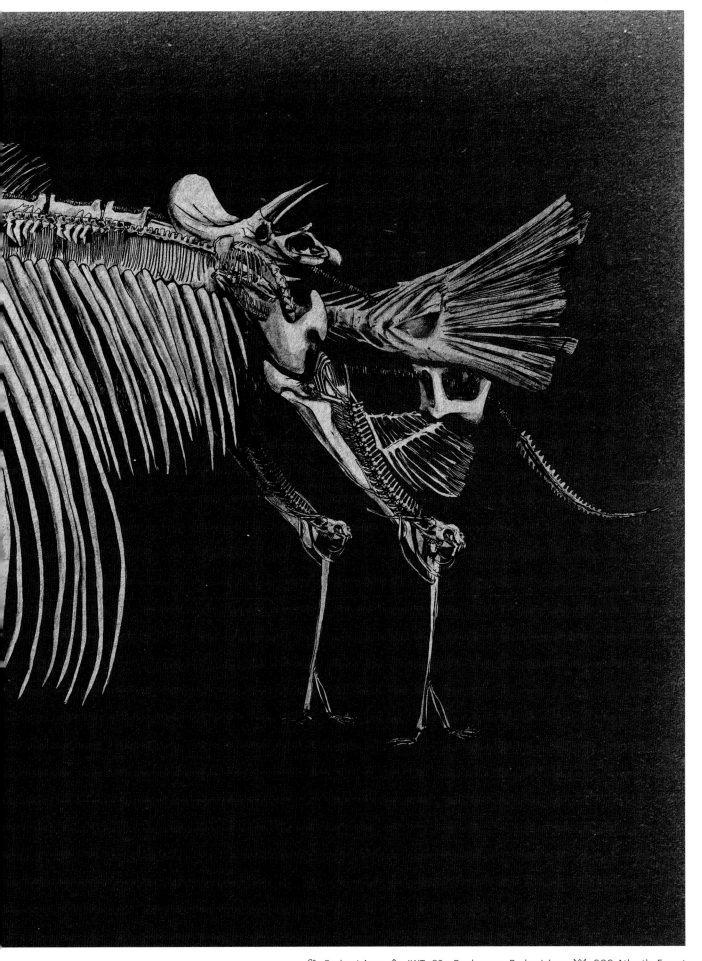

☺: Pedro Izique ᴀ: JWT, São Paulo ⊏⊐: Pedro Izique ♕: SOS Atlantic Forest

©: Anson Liaw ♔: Mercatto

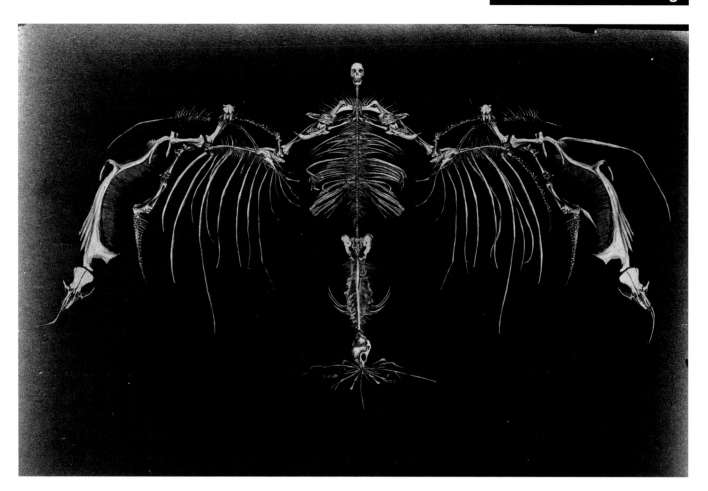

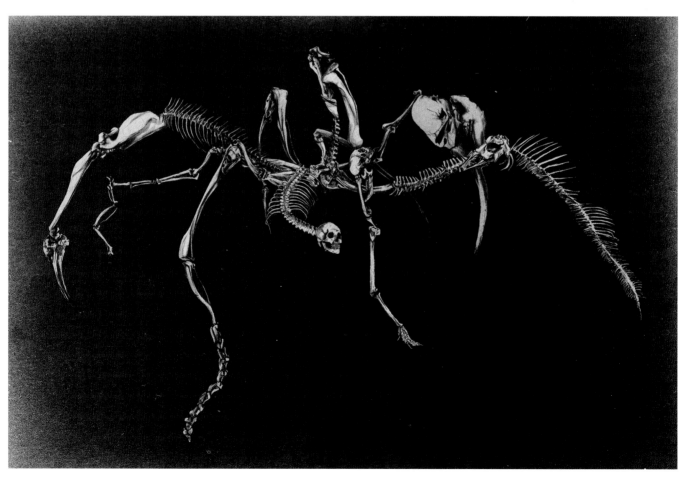

☺: Pedro Izique ☝: JWT, São Paulo ☞: Pedro Izique ♔: SOS Atlantic Forest

☺: Eszter Kiskovacs ♛: Self-promotion

C: 2FRESH A: 2FRESH ♛: Grafuck

✐: Caglar Biyikoglu ♕: Self-promotion

✐: Andrew Bannecker ♕: Self-promotion

✐: Ron Monnier ♕: Self-promotion

©: Mark Joseph Deutsch ⌂: Happy Garaje, Cebu ♛: Xlibris

©: Kim Rosen ♛: Self-promotion

©: Brock Davis ♛: Threadless

⌚: Eduardo Casassus ⌂: Agencia Mostro, Santiago ✏: Daslav Maslov, Eduardo Casassus ♛: nosotrasquenosqueremostanto.cl

⌚: Daniel Malecki/ExDandy ♛: Sas&Lou Hairdressing Salon, Sydney

☻: Craig McGill ⌂: Draftfcb, Melbourne ♛: Honda

☻: Eduardo Tavares ⌂: Exclam, Curitiba, Brazil ▭: Eduardo Tavares ♛: Olé Spanish Restaurant

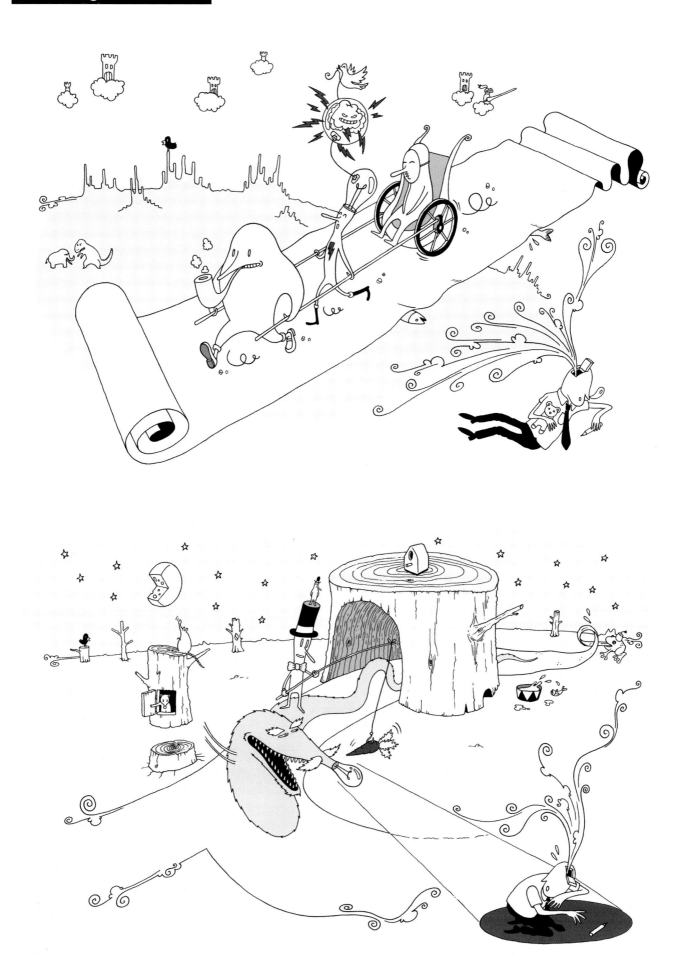

☺: Brosmind Studio ☖: Villarrosas, Barcelona ♕: Honda

©: Justin Gabbard ♛: Gutter Comics

©: James O'Brien ♛: Veer

©: Jon Krause ♛: ACM

⊙: Justin Gabbard ♕: Self-promotion

⊙: Frank Stockton ♕: Intelligence Report

☻: Shane Luskie ♕: Hangoversquare

⏱: Chris Judge 🖎: Richard Seabrooke 👑: Candy

⏱: Chris Judge ⌂: DDFH&B/JWT, Dublin 🖎: Mark Shanley 👑: Vodafone

⏱: Chris Judge ⌂: McConnells, Dublin 🖎: Aileen Coonan 👑: BMW Mini

⏱: Chris Judge 🖎: Darren McCreesh 👑: Maximum Joy

☺: Eduardo Bertone ♛: Anna Goodson Management

☺: Max Ellis ♛: Lloyds Bank

☺: Edvard Scott ♛: Wellcome Trust

☺: Lomp ♛: Self-promotion

☺: Alex Zoebisch 👑: Self-promotion

75

☻: Alexandre Norito Miyaki ⌂: Exclam, Curitiba, Brazil ♕: Ciranda

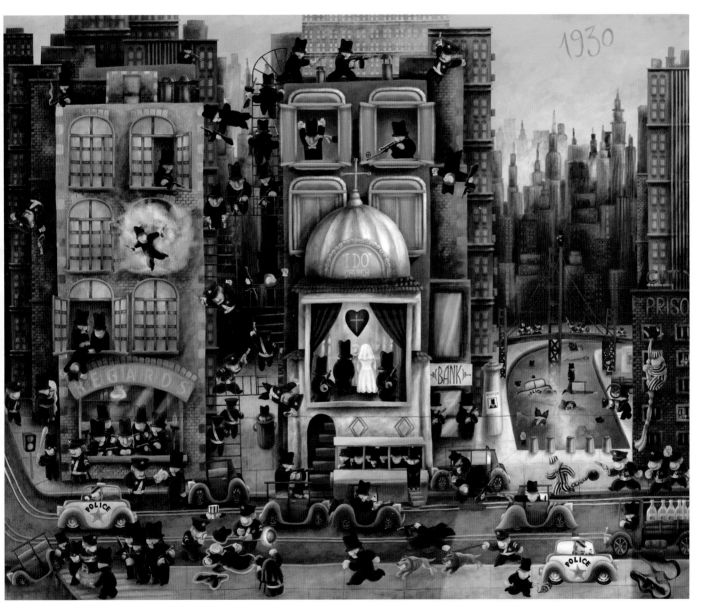

☻: Vali Petridean ♕: Self-promotion

☺: Sunil Garud ⌒: Bluecockroach, Mumbai ♕: Salaam Bombay Foundation

☺: Eelco van den Berg ♕: Bacardi

🕐: Jan Feindt 👑: RitterSlagman\VFL Gummersbach

Ⓒ: Jan Feindt ♔: BASF

☺: Pedro Izique ⌂: JWT, São Paulo ▭: Pedro Izique ♔: Gazeta Mercantil

 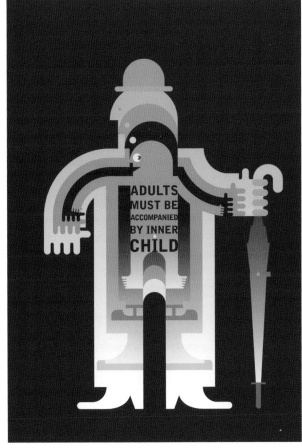

☺: Paul Pateman ⌂: Abbott Mead Vickers BBDO, London
♔: Museum of Childhood

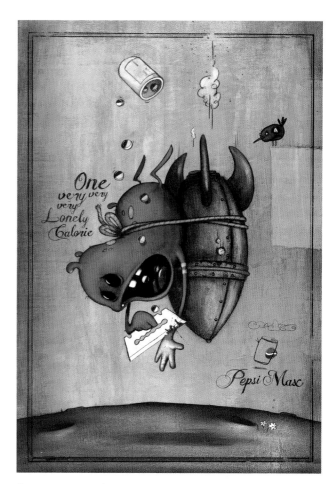

☺: Johan Potma ⌂: BBDO, Düsseldorf ▭: Michael Plückhahn, Kenny Blumenschein ♛: Pepsi Max

☺: Johan Potma ♛: Interned Services

☺: Abhishek Sawant ☽: Zeuss Home Foodz

THIS IS THE PRICE YOU COULD PAY
FOR WORKING ABROAD ILLEGALLY.

International
Organization
for Migration
www.iom.org.ua

Ⓒ: Pavel Klubnikin Ⓐ: Leo Burnett, Kiev Ⓦ: International Organization for Migration

Ⓒ: Freddy Jana Ⓐ: Saatchi & Saatchi, New York ▭: Freddy Jana, Frank Fusco Ⓦ: Toyota

©: Page Tsou ♡: Taiwan Art Education Center

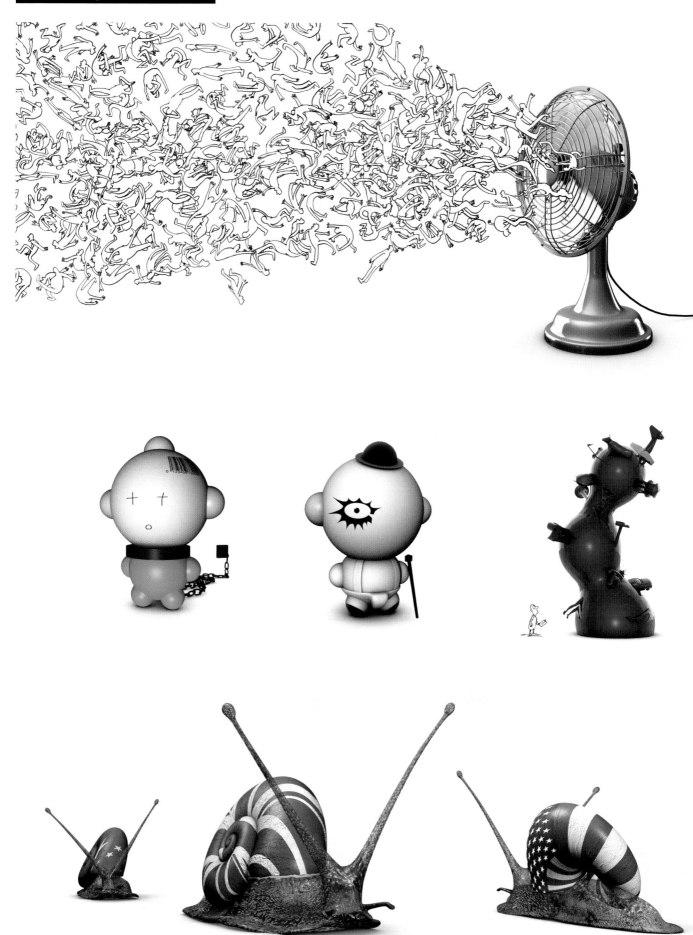

☺: artbombers ♛: Self-promotion

⏱: Alessandro Adelio Rossi ♕: Frameevents

©: Thomas Simpfendoerfer ⌂: Euro RSCG Worldwide, New York ▭►: Bill Previdi ♔: Astellas Pharma

☺: Carioca ⌂: Saatchi & Saatchi, Bucharest ♛: Greenpeace

⌚: Kleber Menezes ♔: Brooklyn Book

Achilles

Son of mortal Peleus, king of the myrmidons, and the immortal sea nymph Thetis in Greek... When Achilles was born Thetis tried to make him by dipping him in the river Styx. However she forgot to wet the heel she held him by leaving him vulnerable at that spot.

The Centaur's Fate

The horse is at the best of his vigour when three years have passed round, not so the boy by any means for men at this time he will often in sleep seek his mother's milky breast. Afterwards, when the strong powers of the horse are failing in old age and his body fronts as life recedes, then is the time of the flower of boyhood, when youth is beginning and is clothing the chin with soft hair.

: Kleber Menezes : BLURB

⊘: Daniel Malecki/ExDandy ♛: Self-promotion

⊘: Erica Dorn ♛: W+K Tokyo Lab

✌: Jamie Williams ♛: Self-promotion

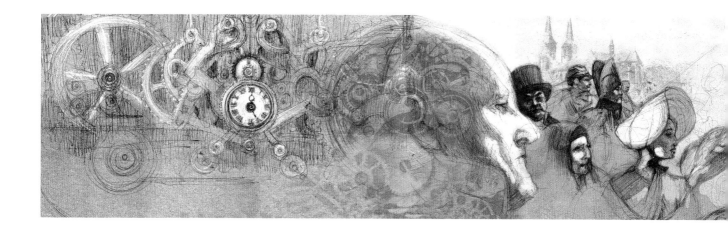

♡: Cathy Gendron ▭: Rita Frangie ♔: The Penguin Gr

☺: David von Bassewitz ♕: HBV HörBild Verlag

☺: Adrià Fruitós ♕: Edicions Hipòtesi

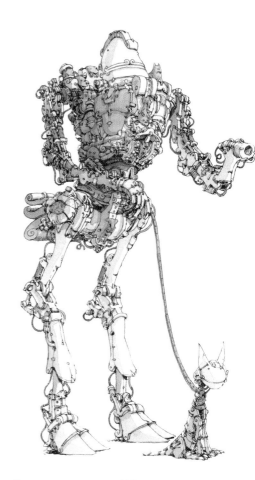

☺: Mattias Adolfsson ♛: Bonnier Carlsen

☺: Mattias Adolfsson ♛: Dance Gavin Dance

☺: Craig McGill ♛: Random House Australia

☻: David Despau ♔: Jaleo DSGN

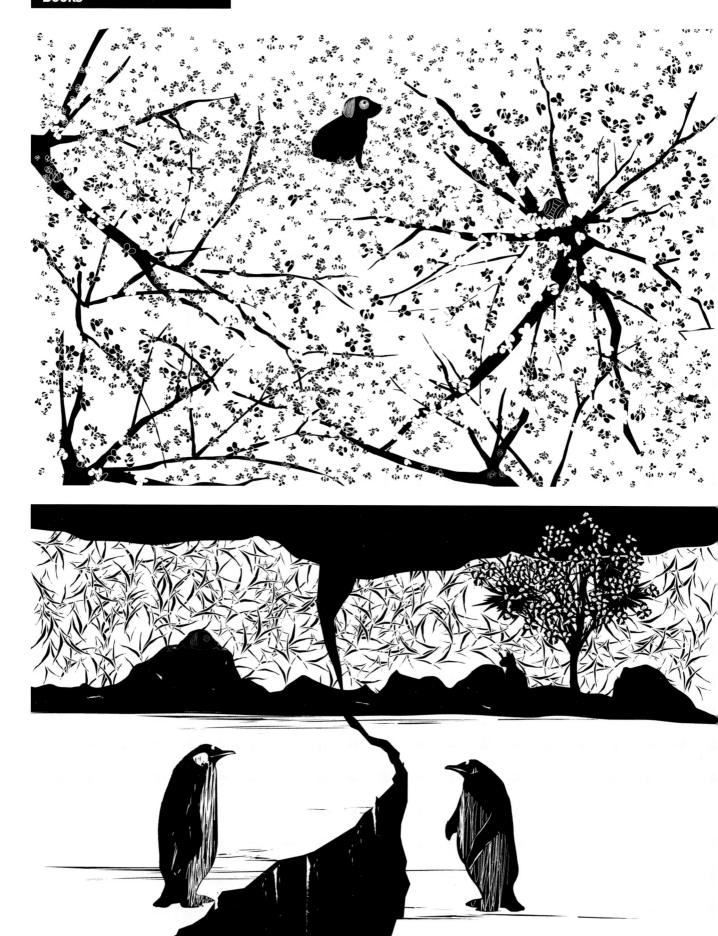

☺: Patray Lui ♛: Cane Picio

☺: Annika Sköld ♛: Liber

☺: Rahele Jomepour ♕: Self-promotion

⚘: Cheri Scholten ♛: Self-promotion

Ⓒ: Anna Cairanti ♔: Topipittori

Ⓒ: Irina Troitskaya ▭: Viktor Melamed ♔: Self-promotion

🕐: Alexandra Zaharova 👐: Art. Lebedev Studio, Moscow 👑: Martini

⌚: Rahele Jomepour 👑: Éditions Courtes et Longues

⌚: Catty Flores 🖌: Pedro Vega 👑: Aquent

⏱: Petra Kolitsch ♔: Self-promotion

⏱: Petra Kolitsch ♔: Eichborn Verlag

☺: Nicolas Bolasini ♙: Editorial Puerto de Palos

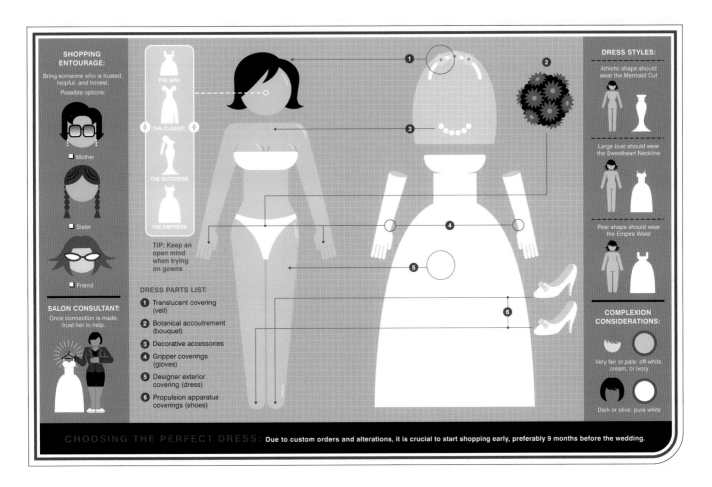

SHOPPING ENTOURAGE:
Bring someone who is trusted, helpful, and honest.
Possible options:
- ☐ Mother
- ☐ Sister
- ☐ Friend

SALON CONSULTANT:
Once connection is made, trust her to help.

TIP: Keep an open mind when trying on gowns

THE MINI
THE CLASSIC
THE DUTCHESS
THE EMPRESS

DRESS PARTS LIST:
1. Translucent covering (veil)
2. Botanical accoutrement (bouquet)
3. Decorative accessories
4. Gripper coverings (gloves)
5. Designer exterior covering (dress)
6. Propulsion apparatus coverings (shoes)

DRESS STYLES:
Athletic shape should wear the Mermaid Cut
Large bust should wear the Sweetheart Neckline
Pear shape should wear the Empire Waist

COMPLEXION CONSIDERATIONS:
Very fair or pale: off-white, cream, or ivory
Dark or olive: pure white

CHOOSING THE PERFECT DRESS: Due to custom orders and alterations, it is crucial to start shopping early, preferably 9 months before the wedding.

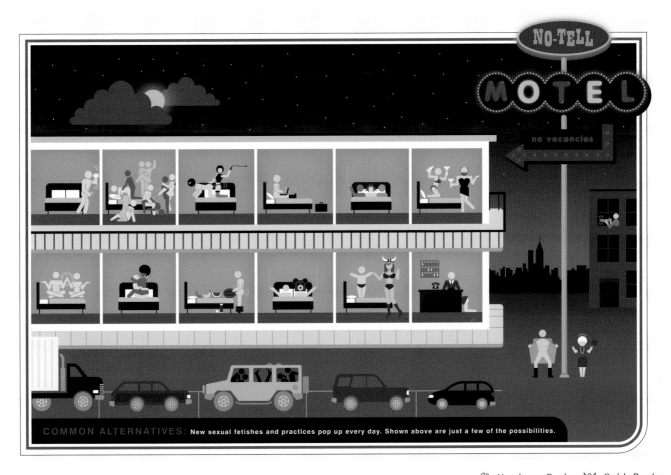

COMMON ALTERNATIVES: New sexual fetishes and practices pop up every day. Shown above are just a few of the possibilities.

Ⓒ: Headcase Design ♕: Quirk Books

⌚: Zsolt Vidak ♛: Moholy-Nagy University of Art and Design Budapest/Roham

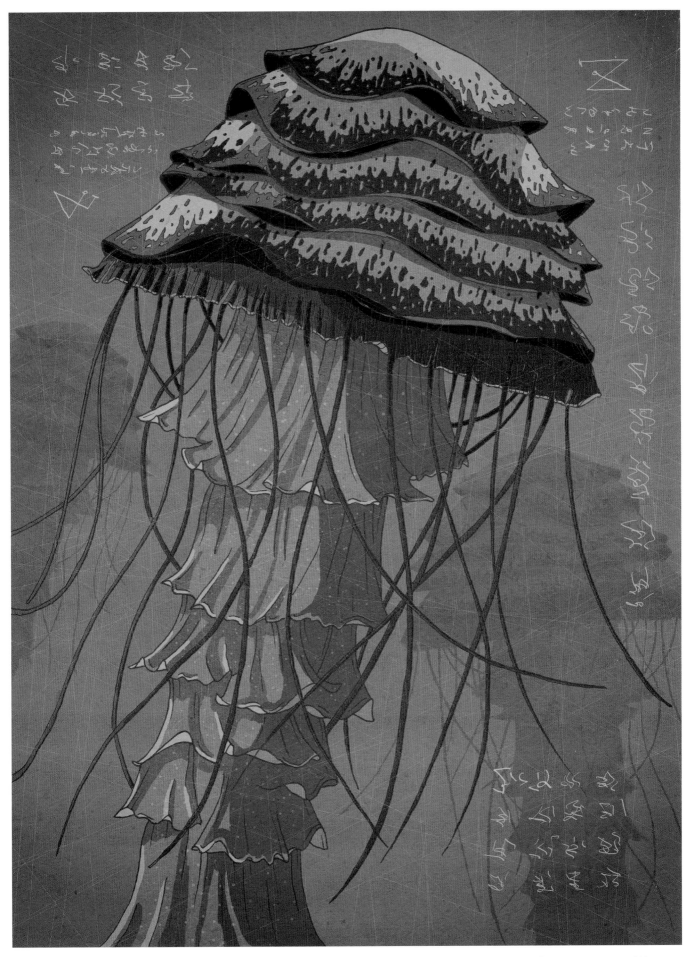

☾: Sergey Steblina ♔: Motto

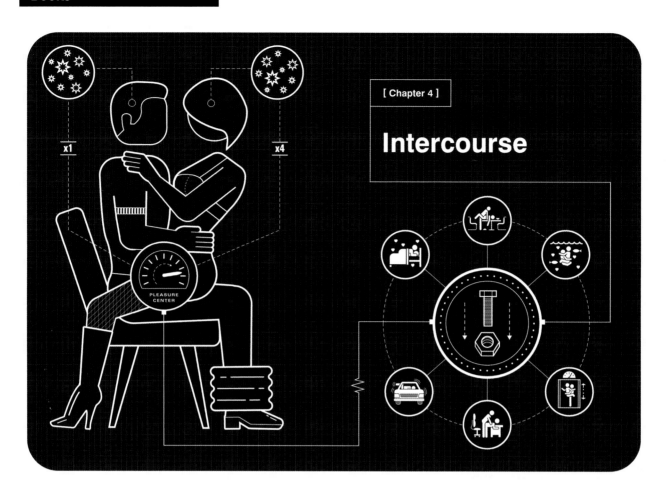

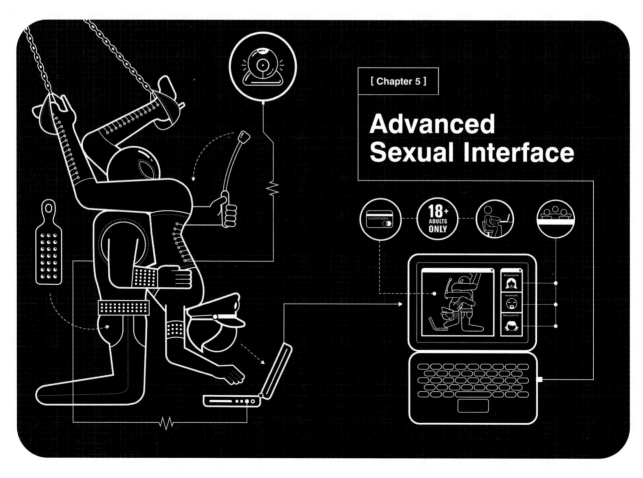

[Chapter 6]

Sexual Accessories

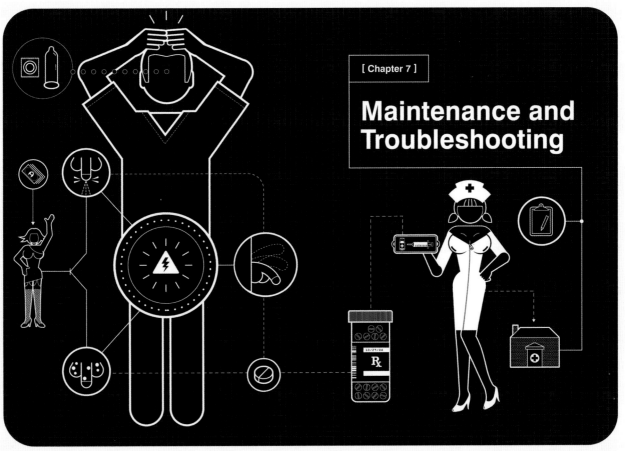

[Chapter 7]

Maintenance and Troubleshooting

☾: Headcase Design ☽: Quirk Books

♔: Tina Berning ♔: Trendbuch

🕐: Kako 👑: Image Comics

☾: Jan Feindt ☙: SSC

☺: Ana Galvan ♕: Die Gestalten Verlag

☺: Noper ♛: Self-promotion

♔: Luca Laurenti ♡: Lascivious

200bil 09.002

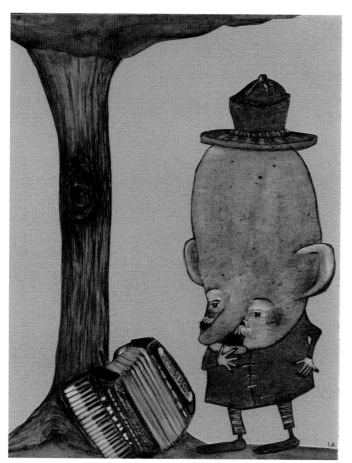

☺: Lisa Kaser ♕: Self-promotion

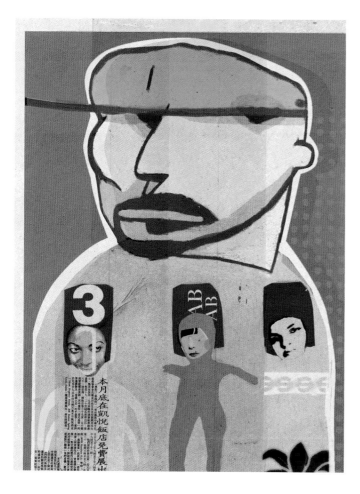

☺: Caglar Biyikoglu ♕: Self-promotion

Kassandra

⏱: Agata Janus 👑: Self-promotion

☺: Julia Bereciartu ♈: Kitchen, Madrid ♛: Fnac

♡: Papriko, Ink. ♕: Self-promotion

TONIGHT DJ SET

⌚: Alessandro Adelio Rossi 👑: aarg, Bergamo

☺: Elisa Sassi ♛: Self-promotion

☉: Jorge Mascarenhas ♔: Self-promotion

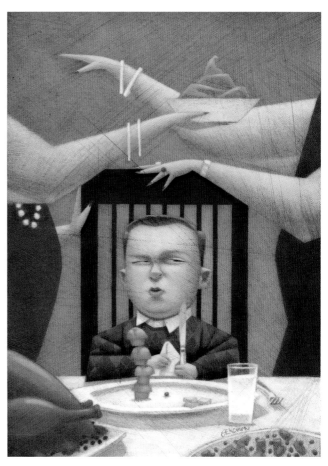

☺: Sean Macfarlane ♛: Self-promotion

☺: Cathy Gendron ♛: Self-promotion

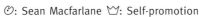

☺: Jennifer Taylor ▭: Michael Quackenbush ♛: Avanti Press

☺: Karol Lasia ♕: BREAK-FAST

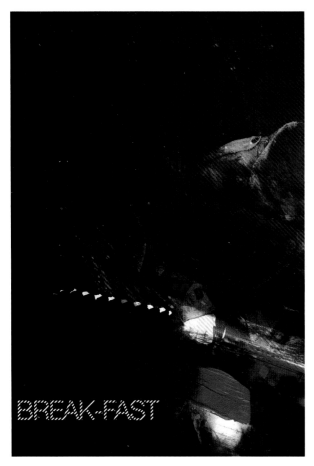

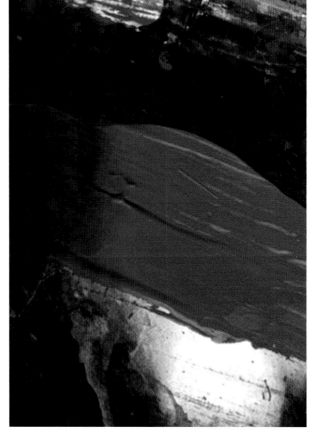

☺: Karol Lasia ♕: BREAK-FAST

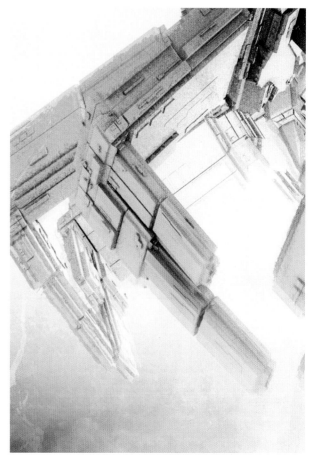

⌚: Karol Lasia ♔: PRSPCt

SUBMERGED
VIOLENCE AS FIRST NATURE 10MOHM

⌚: Karol Lasia ♔: Submerged

♔: Caglar Biyikoglu ♙: Self-promotion

⏱: Hayato Jome ♔: Self-promotion

☺: Caglar Biyikoglu ♕: Self-promotion

☺: Alexander Grigorev ♕: Self-promotion

🕐: Chris Roth 👑: Self-promotion

✐: David Ho ♕: Seether

☺: Sean Mosher-Smith ▭: Echo Designlab ♛: A Fine Frenzy

☺: Andres Henao ⌒: Accentmarketing, Coral Gables ♛: Music a la Carte

✍: Vika Prokopaviciute ♛: Fortek Records

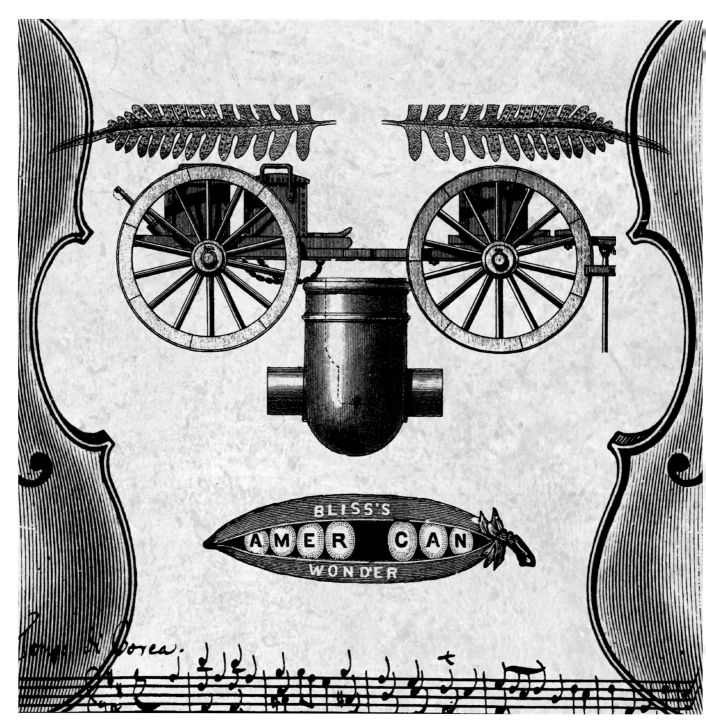

☺: Jim Cohen ♕: Studio Matter

⦵: Dan Smith ⋀: Engine Creative ♛: Renaissance

⏲: Hayato Jome 🌷: Hakushin-Do

℧: James Gulliver Hancock ▭▸: Lizzy Bromley ♛: Simon & Schuster

℧: Tanja Székessy ▭▸: Inka Baron ♛: Das Magazin

THE POISONS OF CAUX

BOOK ONE

the HOLLOW BETTLE

SUSANNAH APPELBAUM

🕐: Jennifer Taylor ▭: Kate Gartner 👑: Random House Young Readers

⌇: Mick Wiggins ♔: Faber and Faber

⌇: Mick Wiggins ♔: Mariner Publishing

⌇: Mick Wiggins ♔: Random House

Ⓒ: Graham Samuels ♕: Pomona Books

⏱: Steven Tabbutt 🔌: Sungyoon Choi 👑: Rabid Rabbit

🖋: Sam Weber 🖊: Nick Jehlen 👑: The Progressive

⌣: Edel Rodriguez ♔: Time

Cover page

☺: Ron Monnier ♛: The Big Issue

PRICE $4.50

THE NEW YORKER

JULY 30, 2007

K

Ⓒ: Anita Kunz Ⓦ: The New Yorker

200bil 09.010

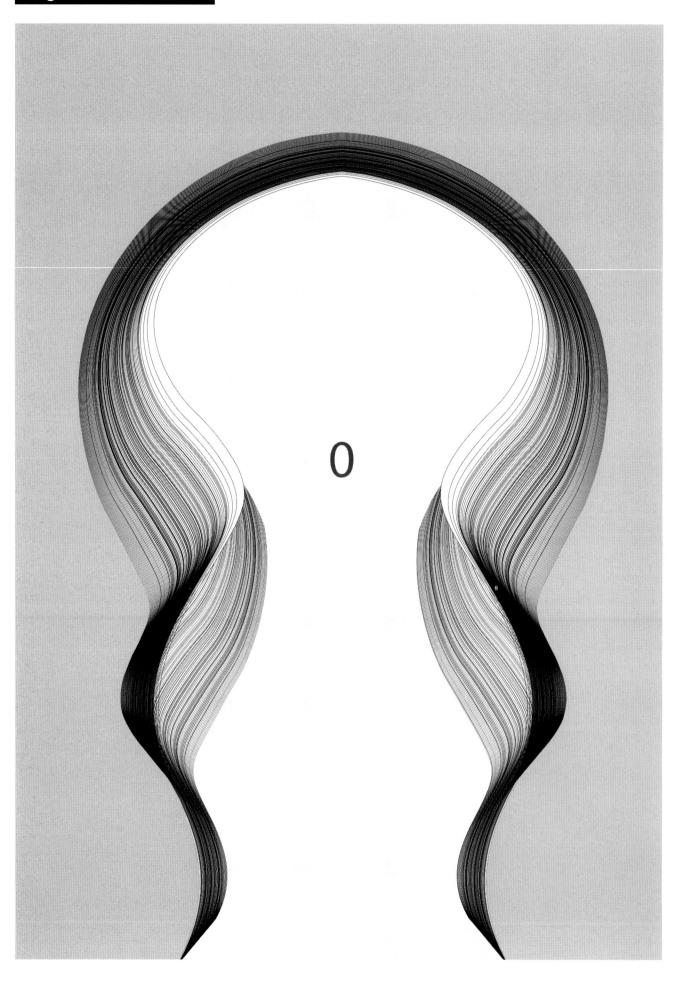

✆: Aleksandra Knezevic ♕: Dixie Magazine

☺: Tanja Székessy ♕: Das Magazin

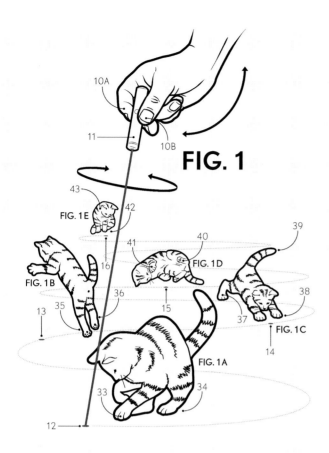

FIG. 1

©: Josh McKible ♔: Spectrum Magazine

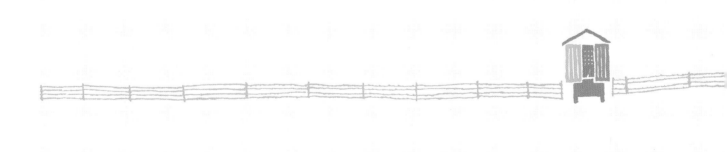

Ⓒ: Alexandra Falagara ♛: The New York Times

Ⓒ: George Bates ♛: The New York Times

©: Mattias Käll ♔: Dagen

Ⓒ: Julia Bereciartu ♔: N.E.E.T. Magazine

Ⓒ: Scott Bakal ♔: Minnesota Magazine

Ⓒ: Viktor Melamed ♕: Inflight Review

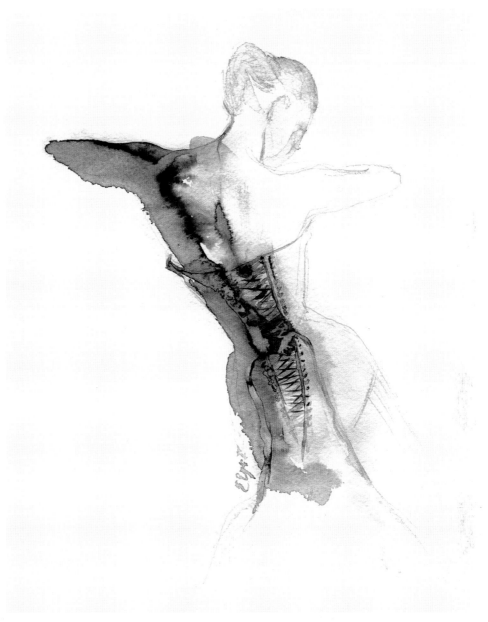

☺: Elena Tsaregradskaya ♕: SOBAKA.ru Magazine

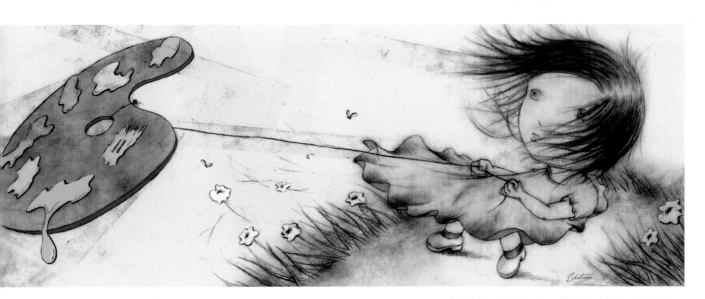

☺: Nathaniel Eckstrom ♕: Australian Art Review

🕒: Anita Kunz 👑: The New Yorker

🕒: Anita Kunz 👑: The New Yorker

🕒: Anita Kunz 👑: Vanity Fair

☺: Noper ♛: Esquire

☺: Kerstin Lindermeier ♛: MySpy Munique

☺: Cathy Gendron ♛: Aspen Magazine

☺: Yihsin Wu 👑: Liberty Times

☺: Juan Carlos Cabadas Reyna 👑: Desfaz Magazine

☺: Yihsin Wu ♛: United Daily News

☺: Yihsin Wu ♛: Liberty Times

©: Daniel Stolle 🖃: Dietmar Dänecke 👑: DIE ZEIT Literatur

©: Daniel Stolle 🖃: Thomas Kartsolis 👑: SZ Wissen

✍: Daniel Stolle 🖊: Bec Brown 👑: Blanket Magazine

✍: Daniel Stolle 🖊: Brigitte Meyer 👑: Neue Zürcher Zeitung Campus

🕐: George Bates 👑: Clarion

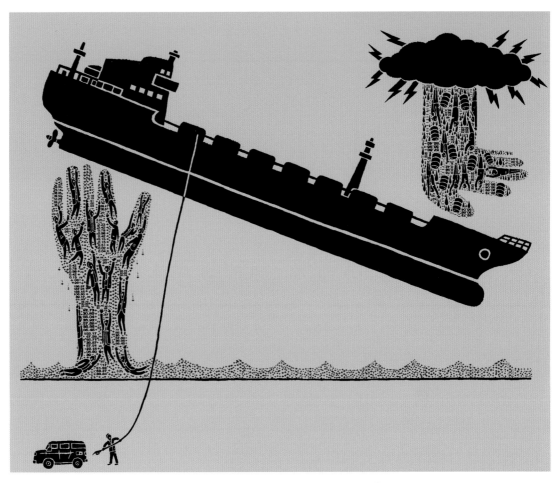

☺: George Bates ♛: Business Week

☺: George Bates ♛: Johns Hopkins Magazine

☺: George Bates ♛: Howies

☺: David von Bassewitz ♕: BBC History Magazine

☺: Jens Bonnke ▭▷: Daniel Bognar ♕: SZ Magazin

©: Anita Kunz ♔: Vanity Fair

☻: Jason Brooks ▭: David Downton ♛: POURQUOI PAS

⌚: Jason Brooks 👜: Jason Brooks 👑: POURQUOI PAS

⌚: Jason Brooks 👜: Dan Baxter 👑: HEDKANDI

⌚: Jason Brooks 🖋: Jason Brooks 👑: HEDKANDI

⌚: Jason Brooks 🖋: Dan Baxter 👑: HEDKANDI

⌚: Jason Brooks 🖉: Jason Brooks 👑: HEDKANDI

⌚: Jason Brooks 🖉: Dan Baxter 👑: HEDKANDI

◔: Lisa Billvik ♕: Habit

◔: Ana Galvan ♕: Saatchi & Saatchi, Madrid

☻: Anne Lück ▭: Amélie Schneider ♔: Jungsheft

Ⓒ: Paola Piglia 👑: Chrismon

☻: Paola Piglia ♔: Chrismon

☺: Pedro Izique ⌂: JWT, São Paulo ▭: Pedro Izique ♕: Gazeta Mercantil

✌: Edward Kinsella III 👑: The Progressive

✌: Edward Kinsella III 👑: Alfred Hitchcock Mystery Magazine

✌: Edward Kinsella III 👑: Philadelphia Weekly

✌: Edward Kinsella III 👑: Alfred Hitchcock Mystery Magazine

☺: Mark Timmins ♖: Engaged Investor Magazine

Ⓒ: Edel Rodriguez ♛: The New Yorker

Ⓒ: Stephen Ledwidge ♛: Security Management Magazine

Ⓒ: Jon Krause ♛: BusinessWeek

☺: Marco Wagner ♛: Playboy

☾: Marco Wagner ▭▷: Heinz Elpermann ♕: Effilee

☾: Marco Wagner ♕: Playboy

✎: Thomas L. Fluharty ♛: The Village Voice

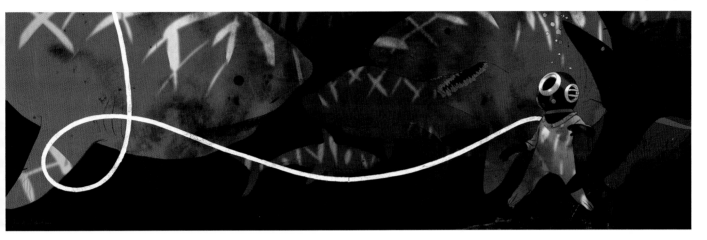

©: Frank Stockton ♛: Plan Advisor Magazine

©: David von Bassewitz ♛: New Scientist

☺: Jennifer Taylor ♕: Orange Life Magazine

☺: Jennifer Taylor ♛: Cosmopolitan

©: David Heatley 🖤: The New Yorker

🕐: Marco Marella 🖂: Ventiquattro Magazine

⏱: Liz Lomax 🖊: Brian Johnson 👑: Minnesota Monthly

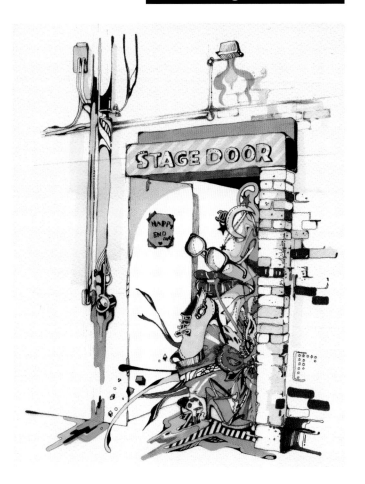

♡: Pomme Chan ♡: Yen Magazine

☺: Jon Krause ♛: LA Times

☺: Jon Krause ♛: Governing

☺: Jon Krause ♛: Washington Post

☺: Jonathan Cusick ♛: The Times

Ⓒ: Mimi Leung ♛: The Guardian

Ⓒ: Vadim Gannenko ⌂: Artmonolit, Dnepropetrovsk ♛: Publishing Diva

⏱: Headcase Design ♛: Fortune Small Business

⏱: Eduardo Bertone ♛: Black Warrior Review

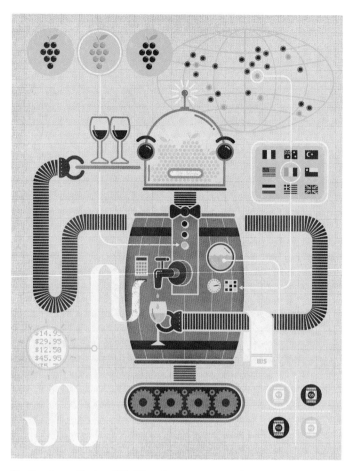

©: Headcase Design ♛: Wine Spectator Magazine

©: Headcase Design ♛: Kiwi Magazine

©: Headcase Design ♛: Newsweek

☺: Headcase Design ♕: The Boston Globe

☺: Jan Feindt ♔: Das Magazin

☺: Jan Feindt ♔: The New York Times

♥: Frank Stockton ♥: Penthouse

◎: Max Ellis ♔: Diver Magazine

◎: Kyle T. Webster ▭: Max Bode ♔: The New Yorker

⏱: Robert Carter 🗀: Tim Kelly 👑: North Shore Magazine

☺: Tymek Jezierski ♕: Piktogram

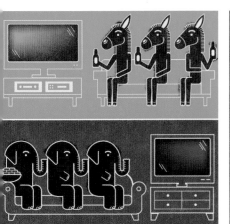

⊙: Headcase Design ♡: The Boston Globe

☻: Mats Bergen ♛: DIVA

⊙: Anja Kroencke ♛: Nippon Vogue

⊘: Joseph Daniel Fiedler ▭▷: Soojin Buzelli ♔: Plansponsor Magazine

⊘: Joseph Daniel Fiedler ▭▷: Jessica Decker ♔: Hour Detroit Magazine

⊘: Joseph Daniel Fiedler ♔: La Luz de Jesus Gallery

⊘: Joseph Daniel Fiedler ▭▷: Mark Murphy/Murphy Design ♔: The Robert Berman Gallery

☺: Matt Murphy ♡: The Independent Arts and Books supplement

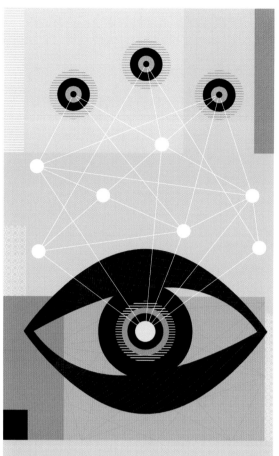

☺: Paul Wearing 🖚: Delilah Zak 👑: The McKinsey Quarterly

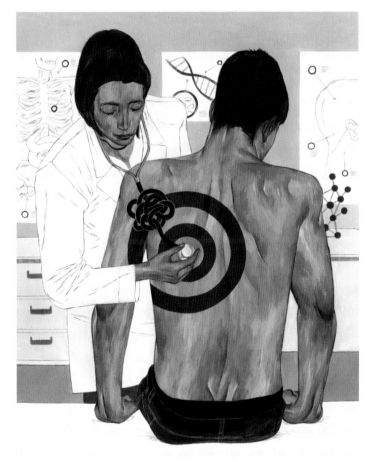

☺: Stephen Ledwidge ♛: Harvard Business Review

✎: Anja Kroencke ♕: easyJet Inflight

☺: Anja Kroencke ♛: Procos

☺: Anja Kroencke ♛: easyJet Inflight

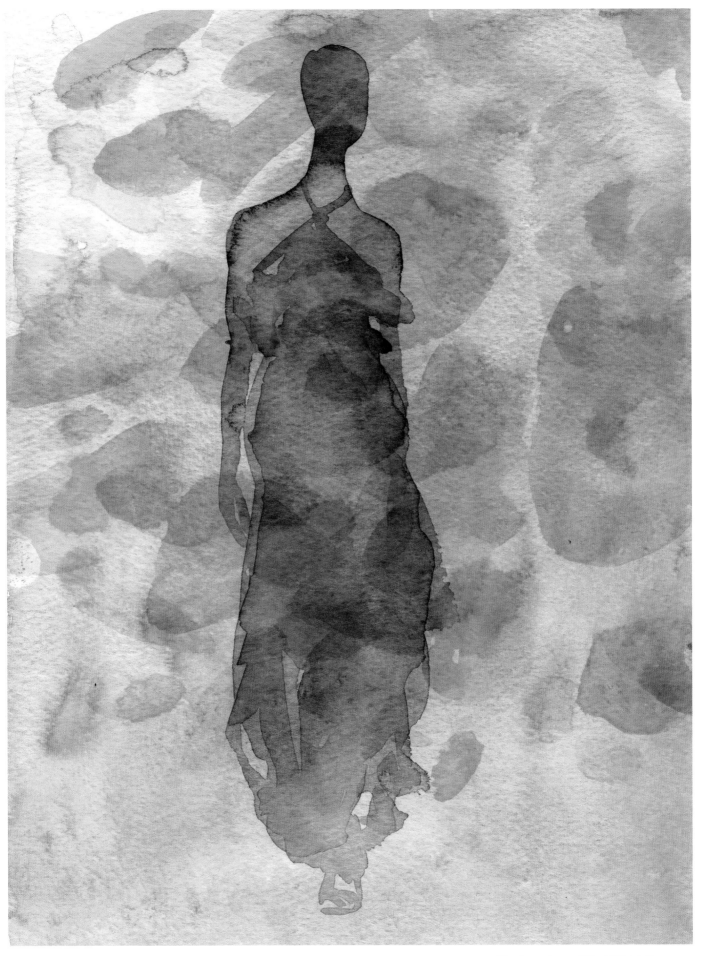

☺: Chuanda Tan ♕: L'Officiel Singapore

☺: Jay Taylor ♛: CPO Agenda

☺: Olaf Hajek ♔: Ritz Carlton

☺: Olaf Hajek ♔: J'N'C Magazine

☺: Olaf Hajek ♔: Süddeutsche Zeitung Magazin

☺: Olaf Hajek ♔: The New York Times

©: David von Bassewitz ♕: HBV HörBild Verlag

200bil 09.002

☺: Scott Bakal ♡: Self-promotion

⌚: Martin Haussmann ⌂: Space5-Design, Cologne ✎: Andrea Härtlein ♕: Bundeszentrale für politische Bildung

Hermann Hesse - Der Steppenwolf

⌚: Martin Haussmann ♕: Westdeutscher Rundfunk

☻: Gili Comforty ♕: Big Brother Wall Prints (The Bathroom) - Kuperman Productions

☺: Gili Comforty ♛: Channel 2

200bil 09.006

⏱: Julia Ziegler ᗩ: Jung von Matt, Hamburg 🖋: Julia Ziegler 👑: Jung von Matt

☺: Sonia Hidalgo Delorme ♕: Raro

EL MILENA RISMO VA A LLEGAR

☺: Sonia Hidalgo Delorme ♕: Raro

☺: PixelPastry 📷: Lim Si Ping (LASALLE College of the Arts) 🍺: Tiger Beer

©: Coen Hamelink ♕: Brabants Instituut voor School en Kunst (BisK)

©: Meike Andresen ♕: Katholische Akademie

©: IC4DESIGN INC./Hirofumi Kamigaki ♔: ©althi Inc./"World Neverland" Online Game Image Visual

200bil 09.012

☾: Daniel Dociu ♔: Arenanet/Guild Wars

☺: Daniel Dociu ♛: Arenanet/Guild Wars

⊙: Coen Hamelink ▭: Renske van Dillen ♛: Brabants Instituut voor School en Kunst (BisK)

⏱: Ivan Maximov ♕: Self-promotion - animation film

⊘: Yuji Yamada ♕: Self-promotion

☺: Abigail McKenzie ♔: Self-promotion

☺: Karol Guerrero ♔: Self-promotion

☺: Irina Grabarnik ♔: Internationale Opera Producties

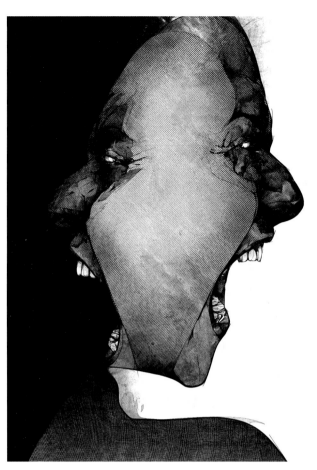

♻: Edward Kinsella III ♛: Self-promotion

♻: Kako ♛: Itaú Cultural

♻: Anita Kunz ♛: Rolling Stone

♻: Anita Kunz ♛: Gallery Hugo

☺: Norbert Horvath ☖: FRIENDLY FIRE, Vienna ♛: Linda Zlok Modedesign

⌖: Showko Akane ♛: Self-promotion

⏱: Sae Tachimori 👑: Self-promotion

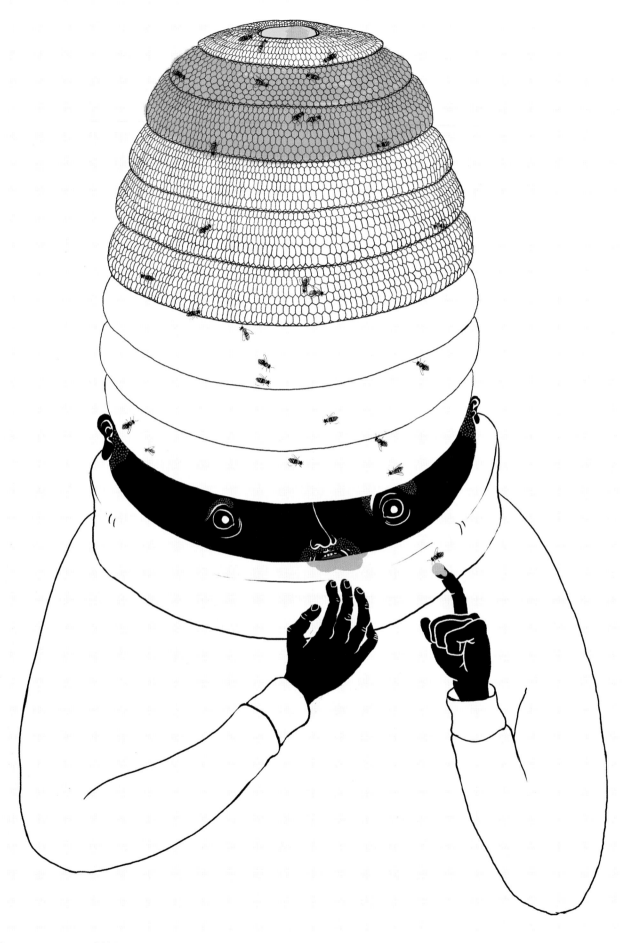

⊙: Santiago Morilla ⊔: Self-promotion

⊘: Santiago Morilla ♕: La-Trastienda Comunicación

⊘: Danijela Dobric ♕: Self-promotion

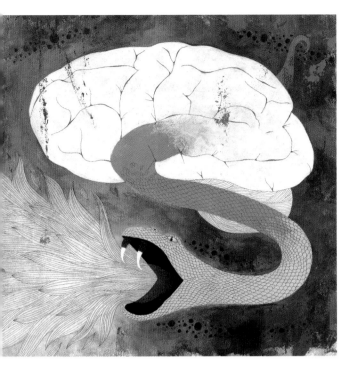

⌚: Scott Bakal ♛: Best Life Magazine

⌚: Scott Bakal ♛: Cut to the Drummer

⌚: Scott Bakal ♛: Self-promotion

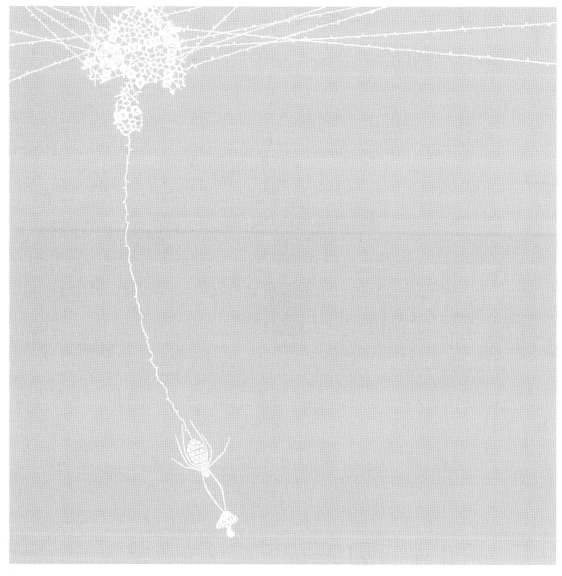

☺: Mitsunari Kawamoto ♕: Self-promotion

◔: Hiromitsu Kobayashi ♕: Self-promotion

⌖: Freddy Jana ♛: Circulo de Educación Integ

⌖: Mogu ♛: Self-promotion

⟲: Sonia Maria Luce ♔: Self-promotion

⟲: Naja Conrad-Hansen ♔: Meannorth

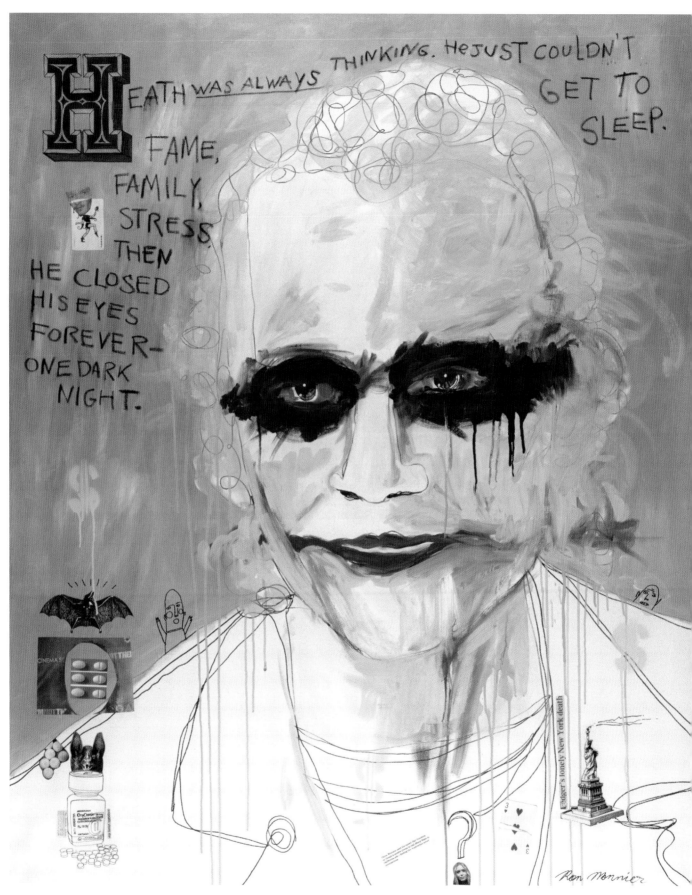

♟: Ron Monnier ♛: Self-promotion

⌒: Hayato Higasa ♛: Self-promotion

⊘: Edel Rodriguez ♔: Soulpepper Theatre

✍: Edel Rodriguez ♛: ICON5

☺: Matteo Franceschini ♔: Young Illustrators Award Contest

✍: Eduardo Bertone ♛: Anna Goodson Management

✍: Carson Ting ♛: Self-promotion

✌: Si Scott ♔: Silent Studios

☾: May Ann Licudine ♕: Self-promotion

: Giulio Iurissevich : Self-promotion

:Tessa Benders : Self-promotion

: Giulio Iurissevich : Grazia Deledda

: Johnny Cheuk : Self-promotion

♔: Olaf Hajek ♕: Self-promotion

⦿: Mimi Leung ♛: Self-promotion

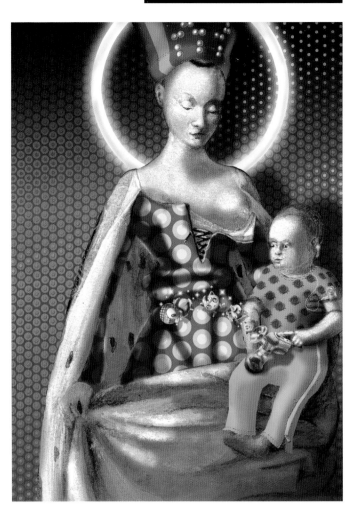

☺: sLip ♕: Self-promotion

☺: Anja Nolte ♕: Self-promotion

☺: Johanna Velasco ♕: Self-promotion

♺: Caroline Stirling ♛: Self-promotion

☺: Thomas L. Fluharty ♛: Self-promotion

200bil 09.029

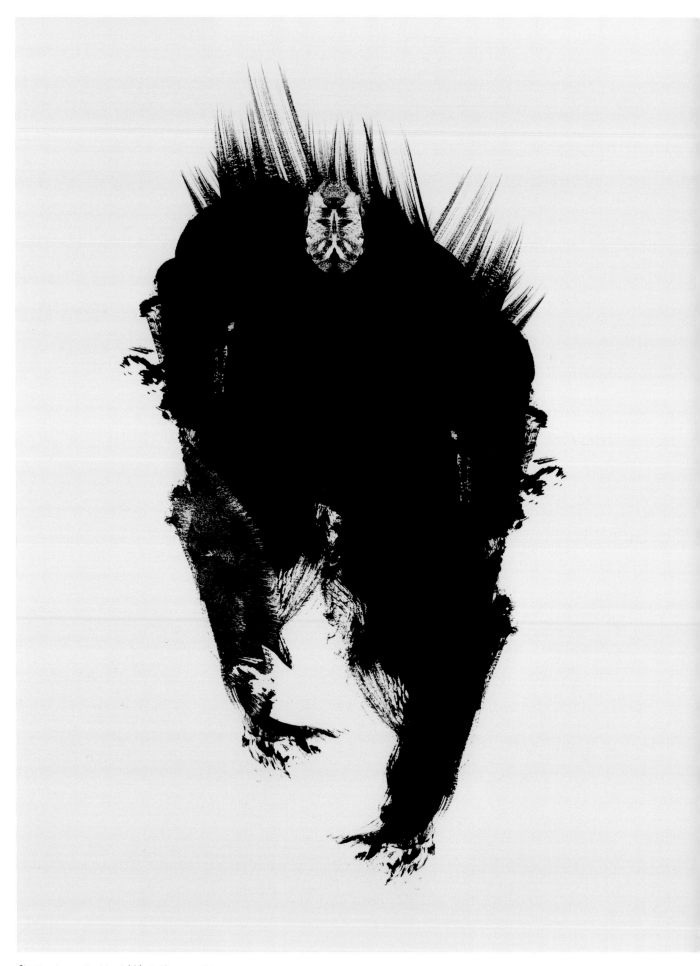

☺: Stephane Goddard ♔: Self-promotion

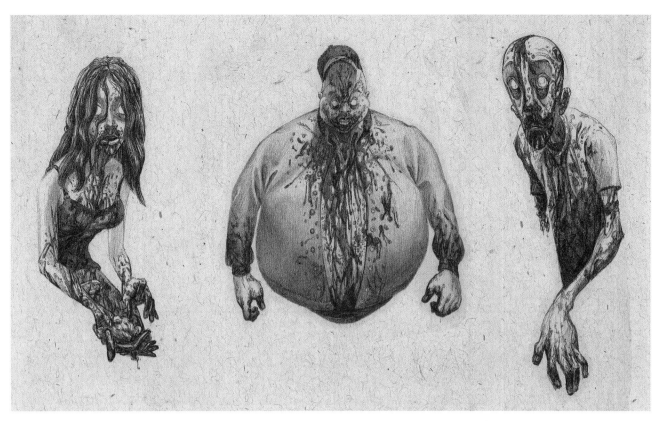

♛: Juan Patino ♛: Self-promotion

♛: Andrew Bannecker ♛: Self-promotion

⏱: Mick Wiggins ♛: The Marin Theatre Company

neryl

☺: Neryl Walker ♡: Self-promotion

☺: Jeff Nishinaka ⌂: KARSH\HAGAN, Denver ⊏▷: Sean Topping ♔: Sprint Press

✍: Ilya Kolesnikov ♛: Post-It Awards '08

⌚: Jasper Wong ▭▶: Michael Sun ♛: Rebel Scholar

☺: Noumeda Carbone ⎘: Francesca Madera ♕: Fantasie

⟲: Jan Feindt ♕: Rosenthal

⟨⟩: Annabelle Jasmin Verhoye ⟨⟩: Malvasia Bianca

☺: Alexandre Norito Miyaki ⌂: Exclam, Curitiba, Brazil ♔: Osmani Guitar Classes

⊙: Tatiana Arocha ♔: The Sundance Channel

2Fresh
Burak, Can
London, United Kingdom
Paris, France
Istanbul, Turkey
email: contact@2fresh.com
canburak@2fresh.com
www.2fresh.com

Adolfsson, Mattias
Sweden
phone: (46) 8 592 503 33
email: mattiasadolfsson@gmail.com
mattiasa.blogspot.com

Akane, Showko
81, Orizu- Hongou
4928071 Inazawa, Aichi
Japan
phone: (81) 1 587 23 61 90
email: showko@lake.ocn.ne.jp
www.sho.ne.jp
jpn-illust.com

Akiyama, Hana
#201 5-10-14, Minamiaoyama
107 0062 Minato-ku, Tokyo
Japan
phone: (81) 3 57 66 46 25
email: info@pict-web.com

Andresen, Meike
Langenfelderstr.43
22769 Hamburg
Germany
email: meike_andresen@gmx.de

Araujo, Carlos
SQSW 105 Bloco A Apt 416, Edifício Via Paris
70670-421 Brasília
Brazil
phone: (55) 61 84 01 29 11
email: carlos@silbachstation.com
www.silbachstation.com

Arocha, Tatiana
Brooklyn, NY
USA
tatiana@servicio-ejecutivo.com
www.tatianaarocha.com
www.ba-reps.com
www.centralillustration.com

Artbombers
The Dispensary, 8 Cleveland Place East
BA1 5DJ Bath
United Kingdom
phone: (44) 20 77 34 71 87
CIA
phone: (44) 207 734 71 87
www.centralillustration.com
Bernstein & Andriulli
phone: (1) 212 682 14 90
www.ba-reps.com

Bakal, Scott
PO Box 531
11722-0531 Central Islip, New York
USA
phone: (1) 888 234 44 92
email: info@scottbakal.com
www.scottbakal.com

Bannecker, Andrew
7131 Arlington Rd, 222
20814 Bethesda, Maryland
USA
phone: (1) 212 6 82 14 90
email: abannecker@gmail.com
www.andrewbannecker.com
www.ba-reps.com

Bates, George
505 Court Street 3B
11231 Brooklyn, New York
USA
phone: (1) 718 573 00 25
email: kingdebris@aol.com
www.georgebatesstudio.com

Benders, Tessa
Graphic design and illustration
Neerbosscheweg 286
6534 BL Nijmegen
The Netherlands
email: tessa@studio-bont.nl
www.studio-bont.nl

Bereciartu, Julia
Marques Viudo de Pontejos 10 4
28012 Madrid
Spain
phone: (34) 62 762 23 31
fax: (34) 91 524 1709
julia@juliabe.com
www.juliabe.com

Bergen, Mats
Eislebener Str. 6
10789 Berlin
Germany
phone: (49) 30 21 91 53 68
mail: matsbergen@t-online.de
www.matsbergen.de
Weinper & Co.
www.weinper.at

Berning, Tina
Artbox › centre for creation
Kruislaan 182
1098 SK Amsterdam
The Netherlands
phone: (31) 20 668 15 51
email: info@artbox.nl
www.artbox.nl

Bertone, Eduardo
Santa Barbara No. 2/4c
Madrid
Spain
phone: (34) 627 94 57 59
email: bertone.eduardo@gmail.com
www.bertoneeduardo.com
Anna Goodson Management
phone: (1) 514 482 04 88
fax: (1) 514 482 06 86
email: info@agoodson.com
www.agoodson.com

Billvik, Lisa
Norrbackagatan 15
11341 Stockholm
Sweden
phone: (46) 739 69 34 90
email: mail@lisabillvik.com
www.lisabillvik.com

Biyikoglu, Caglar
Turkey
phone: (90) 533 359 24 60
email: caglarbiyikoglu@gmail.com
www.caglarbiyikoglu.com

Bolasini, Nicolas
Juncal 4244 - Villa Ballester
1653 Buenos Aires
Argentina
phone: (54) 11 47 64 46 79
fax: (54) 15 55 06 93 99
email: nicolasbolasini@gmail.com
info@nicolasbolasini.com.ar
www.nicolasbolasini.com.ar

Bonnke, Jens
phone: (49) 17 05 86 93 60
email: jb@jensbonnke.de
www.jensbonnke.de

Briers, Stuart
London
phone: (44) 20 86 77 62 03
email: stuart@stuartbriers.com
www.stuartbriers.com

Brooks, Jason
email: jason@jason-brooks.com
www.jason-brooks.com
Folio
10, Gate Street
Lincoln's Inn Fields
WC2A 3HP
London
www.folioart.co.uk
email: all@folioart.co.uk
phone: (44) 207 24 29 56

Brosmind Studio
Alejandro & Juan Mingarro
Passeig Colom 23, 60, 4a
8002 Barcelona
Spain
phone: (34) 933 02 06 32
email: alejandro@brosmind.com
www.brosmind.com

Burke, Bernadette
36 Girraween Crescent
VIC 3064 Craigieburn
Australia
phone: (61) 405 27 59 80
email: bburke@y7mail.com
www.redbubble.com/people/snoopybub

Cabadas, Juan Carlos
Norte #25 no. 26 Nueva Vallejo
7750 D.F. México
México
phone: (52) 5 719 63 83
email: juckr@yahoo.com

Cairanti, Anna
Viale Lombardia 23
20131 Milan
Italy
phone: (39) 333 40 71 552
email: annacairanti@tiscali.it

Canetti, Michel
26 Prospect Hill Road, Camberwell
3124 Victoria
Australia
phone: (61) 3 98 82 94 09
email: canetti@netspace.net.au
www.michelcanetti.com
Representative France: Marie Bastille
www.mariebastille.com
Representative Germany: Margarethe Hubauer
www.margarethe-illustration.com

Carbone, Noumeda
Via dei Serragli 122
50124 Florence
Italy
phone: (39) 338 71 63 604
email: noumeda@inknou.it
www.inknou.it

Carioca
93-95 Lanariei
Bucharest
Romania
phone: (40) 31 405 55 04
email: studio@carioca.ro
www.carioca.ro

Carter, Robert
Cracked Hat Illustration
50 Erbach Crescent
N3A 2L3 Baden, Ontario
Canada
phone: (1) 519 634 83 70
email: rob@crackedhat.com
www.crackedhat.com

Casassus, Eduardo
Penalolen - Av Jose Arrieta 9675-D
Santiago
Chile
phone: (56) 2 279 12 20
email: eduardo.casassus@gmail.com
ecasassus@proximity.cl
www.eduardocasassus.com

Chan, Pomme
A203 Jam Factory, 27 Greenwalk
SE1 4TT
London
United Kingdom
phone: (44) 79 20 13 20 38
email: pomme.chan@gmail.com
www.pommepomme.com
Representative UK: AgencyRush
www.agencyrush.com
phone: (44) 12 73 67 51 22
Representative USA: Friend and Johnson
www.friendandjohnson.com
phone: (1) 212 337 00 55

Cheuk, Johnny
Hong Kong
phone: (85) 260 78 99 41
email: contact@johnnycheuk.com
www.johnnycheuk.com
www.acidbird.com

Cohen, Jim
107 Miller Rd
60047 Hawthorn Woods
USA
phone: (1) 847 726 89 79
email: jim@jimcohenillustration.com
www.jimcohenillustration.com

Comforty, Gili
Droyanov 1 St.
63346 Tel Aviv
Israel
phone: (97) 25 45 29 70 12
email: info@gilicomforty.com
gili.comforty@gmail.com
www.gilicomforty.com

Conrad-Hansen, Naja
Denmark
phone: (45) 22 53 85 40
email: info@meannorth.com
info@meannorth.com
www.anjawiroth.com
www.debutart.com
www.2dm.it

Cusick, Jonathan
United Kingdom
phone: (44) 182 75 00 03
email: theboss@jonathancusick.com
www.jonathancusick.com

Davis, Brock
Carmichael Lynch
110 North 5th street
55403 Minneapolis, Minnesota
USA
phone: (1) 612 334 60 00
email: brockdavis@mac.com
www.itistheworldthatmadeyousmall.com

Despau, David
Falcinelo 27, Atico A
28025 Madrid
Spain
phone: (34) 676 21 61 98
email: david@despau.es
www.despau.com

Deutsch, Mark Joseph
35-E Amon Court Salinas Drive Lahug Cebu
6000 Cebu
Philippines
phone: (63) 92 36 23 73 67
Fax: (63) 91 64 77 38 31
email: deutsch.mj@gmail.com
mark.poorboys.org

Dobric, Danijela
Katarina Bangata 62, 2TR
116 39 Stockholm
Sweden
phone: (46) 768 53 49 94
email: mail@danisdrawings.com
www.danisdrawings.com

Dociu, Daniel
19002 NE 127th Street
98052 Redmond, Washington
USA
phone: (1) 425 443 01 79
email: daniel@arena.net
www.tinfoilgames.com

Dorn, Erica
London
United Kingdom
email: info@erica-dorn.com
www.erica-dorn.com

Duyker, Marloes
Artbox › centre for creation
Kruislaan 182
1098 SK Amsterdam
The Netherlands
phone: (31) 20 668 15 51
email: info@artbox.nl
www.artbox.nl

Eckstrom, Nathaniel
Sydney
Australia
phone: (61) 2 425 33 92 68
email: info@nathanieleckstrom.com
www.nathanieleckstrom.com

Ellis, Max
London
United Kingdom
phone: (44) 20 89 77 89 24
email: max@junkyard.co.uk
www.junkyard.co.uk
CIA
phone: (44) 20 77 34 71 87
www.centralillustration.com/
Bernstein & Andriulli
phone: (1) 212 682 14 90
www.ba-reps.com

Elorza, Joseba
C/ Florida N66 5D
1004 Vitoria
Spain
phone: (34) 665 73 05 56
email: info@miraruido.com
www.miraruido.com

Falagara, Alexandra
Sweden
phone: (46) 739 24 25 18
email: post@alexandrafalagara.com
www.alexandrafalagara.com

Feindt, Jan
Oderberger Straße 54
10435 Berlin
Germany
phone: (49) 30 428 013 73
email: janfeindt@gmx.de
www.janfeindt.de
www.rappart.com
www.plnmanagement.com

Fiedler, Joseph Daniel
2632 Pinewoods Road
95959 Nevada City, California
U.S.A.
email: fiedler@scaryjoey.com
www.scaryjoey.com

Flores, Catty
Richmond, London
United Kingdom
email: catty@ohgrafica.com
www.cattyflores.com

Floship
Unit G, 23/F, Blk 1
Grandeur Terrace
88 Tin Shui Rd
Tin Shui Wai, NT
Hong Kong
phone: (852) 96 09 04 22
email: floship@gmail.com
www.studiofloship.com

Fluharty, Thomas L.
Prior Lake, Minnesota
USA
email: theflus@integra.net
www.thomasfluharty.com

Franceschini, Matteo
Via Fabio Filzi 6
21013 Gallarate
Italy
phone: (39) 03 31 78 29 83
cell phone: (39) 348 767 31 54
email: matteofrances@libero.it
www.associazioneillustratori.it
www.ultra-book.org

Fruitòs, Adriá
6, Rue Saint Ludan
67100 Strasbourg
France
phone: (33) 369 81 57 99
email: adria@fruitosscp.com
www.adfruitos.com

Gabbard, Justin
200 Second Avenue, 24
10003 New York
USA
email: jg@justingabbard.com
www.justingabbard.com

Galvan, Ana
Av. Infante J. Manuel, 7 - T. gemin, 1A
30011 Murcia
Spain
phone: (34) 657 23 41 19
email: ana@anagalvan.com
www.anagalvan.com

Gannenko, Vadim
152 Raboshya Str., Apt. 247
49008 Dnepropetrovsk
Ukraine
phone: (38) 095 767 50 80
email: vadimgannenko@gmail.com
www.artmonolit.com

Garud, Sunil
1/C, 103, Devratna Nagar, Swadeshi Mill Road
4000 022 Sion-Chunabhatti, Mumbai
India
phone: (91) 22 24 05 11 56
phone: (91) 98 19 93 24 83
email: sunilgarud@gmail.com
www.sunilgarud.com
Shiva Anandam
www.bluecockroach.com

Gendron, Cathy
Ann Arbor, Minnesota
USA
email: cathy@cathygendron.com
www.cathygendron.com

Goddard, Stéphane
24 Rue du Chateau Landon
75010 Paris
France
phone: (33) 674 92 80 19
email: contact@stephanegoddard.com
www.stephanegoddard.com

Grabarnik, Irina
Arthur van Schendelplein 103,
2624 CT, Delft
The Netherlands
phone: (31) 628 48 15 35
email: irina@ivgdesign.nl
www.ivgdesign.nl

Grigorev, Alexander
Naberejnaya Fontanki st. 123-506
Saint-Petersburg
Russia
phone: (7) 911 747 23 49
email: sasha@grigorev.com
www.grigorev.com

Guerrero, Karol
Chile 675
1098 Buenos Aires
Argentina
phone: (54) 11 43 62 92 13
Email: info@karolguerrero.com
www.karolguerrero.com
Editorial Trescabezas
www.editorialtrescabezas.com

Hajek, Olaf
Schröderstraße 4
10115 Berlin
Germany
phone: (49) 151 21 24 85 46
email mail@olafhajek.com
www.olafhajek.com
www.boutique-art.com
www.2agenten.com

Hamelink, Coen
Coenmeteenc
Amsterdamsestraatweg 433
3553 EA Utrecht
Denmark
phone: (31) 62 826 79 82
email: coen@coenmeteenc.nl
www.coenmeteenc.nl

Hancock, James Gulliver
Los Angeles, California
USA
email: james@jamesgulliverhancock.com
www.jackywinter.com
www.jamesgulliverhancock.com

Harrold, Geoff
208 Lampits
EN11 8DU Hoddesdon
United Kingdom
phone: (44) 19 92 44 39 04
email: geoff.harrold@ntlworld.com
www.geoffharrold.com
www.geoffsfolly.com

Hashimoto, Takahisa
Yebisu Garden Place 25F,
Ebisu, Shibuya-ku
150-6025 Tokyo
Japan
phone: (81) 3 57 91 86 82
email: contact@takahisahashimoto.com
www.takahisahashimoto.com

Haussmann, Martin: Illustration
Regentenstraße 59
51063 Köln (Mülheim)
Germany
phone: (49) 221 964134 0
martin@haussmann-illu.de
www.haussmann-illu.de

Headcase Design
Philadelphia, Pennsylvania
USA
email: headcase@headcasedesign.com
www.headcasedesign.com

Heatley, David
85-1 34th Ave. 314
11372 Jackson Heights, New York
USA
phone: (1) 347 306 0880
email: davidmheatley@gmail.com

Henao, Andres
Accent Marketing
800 Douglas Road
33160 Coral Gables, Florida
USA
email: ahenao@accentmarketing.com
www.accentmarketing.com

Hidalgo Delorme, Sonia
Rosendo Conde, 17 2ºD
28029 Madrid
Spain
phone: (34) 606 15 55 63
email: info@soniahidalgo.com
www.soniahidalgo.com

Higasa, Hayato
2-8-1 Nishitenma Kita-Ku
530 0047 Osaka
Japan
phone: (81) 06 63 16 73 63
email: info@pict-web.com
http://sunbrella-sakura.ne.jp
PICT
www.pict-web.com

Ho, David
Fremont, California
USA
email: ho@davidho.com
www.davidho.com

Horvath, Norbert
Margaretenstr. 41-43
1040 Vienna
Austria
phone: (43) 676 844 93 61 00
email: n.horvath@friendlyfire.at
Friendly Fire – 3D Concept House
email: frontdesk@friendly.at
ww.friendlyfire.at

Iurissevich, Giulio
Artbox › centre for creation
Kruislaan 182
1098 SK Amsterdam
The Netherlands
phone: (31) 20 668 15 51
email: info@artbox.nl
www.artbox.nl

Izique, Pedro
Mario Amaral, 50
04002-020 São Paulo
Brazil
phone: (55) 11 38 88 80 00
email: pedronline@uol.com.br
pedro.izique@jwt.com
palmeida.blogspot.com

Jana, Freddy
USA/Dominican Republic
email: freddyjana@gmail.com
www.freddyjana.com

Janus, Agata
ul. Woloska 82/34
02-507 Warsaw
Poland
phone: (48) 502 43 15 42
email: gagatka27@hotmail.com
gagatka27@o2.pl
www.gagatka.pl

Jezierski, Tymek
Ul. Mlynarska 25b/22
Warsaw
Poland
phone: (48) 695 59 86 95
email: tymek.jezierski@gmail.com
www.brothersinarms.com.pl

Jome, Hayato
Hayato Jome Unlimited
2-28-1-402, Jingu-mae
150-0001, Shibuya-ku, Tokyo
Japan
email: jome@j.email.ne.jp
www.peacecard.com/jome.html

Jomepour, Rahele
Box No: 14395-198
Tehran
Islamic Republic of Iran
phone: (98) 91 92 40 65 60
email: info@rahelejomepour.com
www.rahelejomepour.com

Judge, Chris
49 Pleasants Street, Side Door
Dublin 8
Ireland
phone: (35) 3 868 15 49 89
email: chrispjudge@gmail.com
www.chrisjudge.com

Kako
Rua Augusta 66, ap09 Consolacao
01304-000 São Paulo
Brazil
phone: (55) 11 21 58 09 65
email: kako@kakofonia.com
www.kakofonia.com
Representative International:
Levy Creative Management
www.levycreative.com
Representative Brazil: Art Pimp
www.artpimp.com.br

Käll, Mattias
Riddarbergsgatan 11
703 68 Örebro
Sweden
phone: (46) 73 509 51 12
email: mattias@mattiaskall.se
info@mattiaskall.se
www.mattiaskall.se

Kamigaki, Hirofumi
IC4DESIGN.INC
1-5 Takayama Bldg 3f, Komachi, Naka-Ku
7300041 Hiroshima
Japan
phone: (81) 82 243 19 99
email: info@ic4design.com
www.ic4design.com

Kaser, Lisa
6411 SE Morrison Ct
97210 Portland, Oregon
USA
email: lisakaser@lisakaser.com
www.lisakaser.com

Kawamoto, Mitsunari
2-8-1 Nishitenma Kita-Ku
530 0047 Osaka
Japan
phone: (81) 06 63 16 73 63
email: info@pict-web.com
www1.ocn.ne.jp/~strobo/
PICT
www.pict-web.com

Kinsella III, Edward
28 Midpark Lane
63124 St. Louis, Missouri
USA
phone: (1) 314 5 83 64 81
email: edwardkinsellaiii@yahoo.com
www.edwardkinsellaillustration.com

Kiskovacs, Eszter
Lovohaz utca 33. III./3
1024 Budapest
Hungary
phone: (36) 13 15 26 20
email: kiskovacs.eszter@gmail.com
www.eszterkiskovacs.com

Kittozutto, Y+J
Block 2, Ghim Moh Road, 05-332
270002 Singapore
Singapore
phone: (65) 98 51 11 45
email: info@kittozutto.com
kittozutto.com

Klubnikin, Pavel
24 Vorovskogo, Building 2, 2nd Floor
1054 Kiev
Ukraine
phone: (38) 677 49 24 20
email: nikbulkin@gmail.com

Knezevic, Aleksandra Nina
Sutjeska 4,
71000 Sarajevo
Bosnia-Herzegovina
phone: (387) 61 27 57 17
email: info@ninadesign.co.ba
www.ninadesign.co.ba
www.ank-ank.com

Kobayashi, Hiromitsu
2-8-1 Nishitenma Kita-Ku
530 0047 Osaka
Japan
phone: (81) 06 63 16 73 63
email: info@pict-web.com
www.hiromitsu-kobayashi.com
PICT
www.pict-web.com

Kolesnikov, Ilya
Lusinovskaya 66-235
115162 Moscow
Russia
phone: (7) 926 579 76 80
email: modest.america@gmail.com
www.modestamerica.com

Kolitsch, Petra
22767 Hamburg
Germany
phone: (49) 40 43 26 93 57
email: kontakt@petra-kolitsch.de
www.petra-kolitsch.de

Krause, Jon
2924 Disston St.
19149 Philadelphia, Pennsylvania
USA
phone: (1) 215 338 1531
email: jk@jonkrause.com
www.jonkrause.com

Kroencke, Anja
129 Grand Street, Apt. 2
10013 New York
USA
phone: (1) 212 34 30 341
email: anja@anjakroencke.com
www.anjakroencke.com

Kunz, Anita
218 Ontario St.
M5A2V5 Toronto
Canada
phone: (1) 416 364 38 46
email: akunz@anitakunz.com
www.anitakunz.com
www.anitakunzart.com

Lasia, Karol
Artbox > centre for creation
Kruislaan 182
1098 SK Amsterdam
The Netherlands
phone: (31) 20 668 15 51
email: info@artbox.nl
www.artbox.nl

Laurenti, Luca
Via Fabiola, 47
00152 Rome
Italy
phone: (39) 340 47 39 755
email: info@mklane.com
www.mklane.com

Ledwidge, Stephen
Dublin, Ireland
email: stephen@stephenledwidge.com
www.stephenledwidge.com
www.agoodson.com

Leung, Mimi
Hong Kong
phone: (85) 266 26 65 87
email: mimi@mimileung.co.uk
www.mimileung.co.uk

Liaw, Anson
Anson Liaw Illustration
325 Highfield Road
M4L 2V4 Toronto, Ontario
Canada
phone: (1) 416 665 65 88
email: ansonliawillustration@rogers.com
www.ansonliaw.com
www.morgangaynin.com

Licudine, May Ann
23 National Highway, Dalumpinas West
2500 San Fernando City
Philippines
phone: (63) 72 242 29 44
email: frecklefaced29@gmail.com
www.mayannlicudine.com

Lindermeier, Kerstin
Paris & Munich
email: kerstin@univers-poetique.com
www.univers-poetique.com

Lomax, Liz
1 Main Street, 7G
11201 Brooklyn, New York
USA
phone: (1) 718 222 5995
email: liz@lizlomax.com
www.lizlomax.com

Lomp
Hermannstraße 24
40233 Düsseldorf
Germany
phone: (49) 211 158 33 54
email: lomp@lomp.de
www.lomp.de

Luce Possentini, Sonia Maria
Via Coppellini 23
42026 Canossa, Reggio Emilia
Italy
phone: (39) 335 56 53 736
email: soniamarialuce@alice.it
www.soniamarialuce.blogspot.com

Lück, Anne
Choriner Str. 52
10435 Berlin
Germany
phone: (49) 30 40 98 75 77
email: welcome@annelueck.com
www.annelueck.com
PLN Management

Lui, Patray
Fokke Simonszstraat 54
1017TJ Amsterdam
The Netherlands
phone: (31) 612 46 14 05
email: info@canepicio.com
www.canepicio.com

Luskie, Shane
43 Waterloo Crescent
3128 Melbourne
Australia
phone: (61) 40 504 98 17
email: design@hangoversquare.com
www.hangoversquare.com

Macfarlane, Sean
Daiichi Hasegawa Biru 302
Takadanobaba 4-14-6
169-0075 Shinjuku-ku, Tokyo
Japan
phone: (81) 90 43 68 76 22
email: sean@illustr8a.com
www.illustr8a.com

Malecki, Daniel/ExDandy
18 Mount Street
NSW 2110 Hunters Hill
Australia
ul. Piastowska 23 20 610 Lublin, Poland
phone: (61) 402 81 82 25
email: exdandy@gmail.com
www.exdandy.com
overallpicture.com

Manero, Alicia
Paseo imperial 19, 2b
28005 Madrid
Spain
phone: (34) 679 93 45 21
email: info@abducida.com
www.abducida.com

Marella, Marco
Cannaregio 6270/b
30121 Venice
Italy
phone: (39) 041 521 01 46
email: marcomarella@gmail.com
www.marcomarella.com
Lilla Rogers Studio
www.lillarogers.com

Mascarenhas, Jorges
1940 Franciscan May, Apt. 216
94501 Alameda, California
USA
phone: (1) 510 3 01 29 34
email: mascarenhas.jorge@gmail.com
www.jorgemstudio.com

Maximov, Ivan
Marshala Novikova 15, 112
123098 Moscow
Russia
phone: (7) 91 04 02 82 57
fax: (7) 95 190 58 90
email: ivan_maximov@mail.ru
www.pipestudio.ru

McGill, Craig
McGill Design Group P/L
PO Box 964
NSW 2039 Rozelle NSW
Australia
phone: (61) 295 55 50 90
fax: (61) 295 55 59 85
email: studio@realnasty.com.au
www.mcgilldesigngroup.com

McKenzie, Abigail
2 Meadows Grove, Codsall
WV8 1GG
Wolverhampton
United Kingdom
phone: (44) 77 31 36 83 29
email: abigailpamela@hotmail.co.uk
www.abigailmckenzie.co.uk

McKible, Josh
Enzo 2-5-19
253-0084 Chigasaki
Japan
phone: (81) 90 11 05 75 75
email: josh@mckibillo.com
www.mckibillo.com

Melamed, Viktor
1-st Monetchikovsky pereulok, 8, 9
115054 Moscow
Russia
phone: (7) 903 710 77 78
email: mlmd@mail.ru
www.mlmd.ru

Meldgaard, Morten
Utopia Design
Copenhagen
Denmark
phone: (45) 27 10 00 80
mail: morten@utopiadesign.dk
www.utopiadesign.dk

Menezes, Kleber
Young & Rubicam
285 Madison Ave
10017-6486 New York
USA
phone: (1) 212 210 3000
email: klebercm@yahoo.com
www.klebercm.com

Metsävainio, Marika
c/o Södra tornet, Slottet ingång H
75325 Uppsala
Sweden
phone: (46) 735 87 93 22
mail: marika@marika-met-art.com
www.marika-met-illustration.com

Modén, Kari
Parkvägen 23
SE-13141 Nacka
Sweden
phone: (46) 704 83 34 50
fax: (46) 8 716 69 11
email: kari@moden.se
www.karimoden.se

Mogu
2-8-1 Nishitenma Kita-Ku Osaka
530 0047 Osaka
Japan
phone: (81) 06 63 16 73 63
email: info@pict-web.com
mogu.boo.jp
vision track
www.pict-web.com

Monnier, Ron
14 Gibson Crescent Holland Park
4121 Brisbane, Qld.
Australia
phone: (61) 7 38 47 84 98
fax: (61) 7 38 47 98 77
email: rmonnier@bigpond.net.au
www.ronmonnier.com.au

Morilla, Santiago
Marqués de Leganés 5, 4D
28004 Madrid
Spain
phone: (34) 91 521 59 23
email: hola@santiagomorilla.com
www.santiagomorilla.com
La Trastienda Comunicación
www.la-trastienda.com

Mosher-Smith, Sean
TheConspiracy
68 Summit St. 2A
11231 Brooklyn, New York
USA
phone: (1) 718 855 4204
email: sean@theconspiracy5.com
www.theconspiracy5.com

Murphy, Matt/Black Coffee Project
Lorna Coldharbour
DT9 4AH Sherborne
United Kingdom
phone: (44) 19 35 81 77 51
email: matt@blackcoffeeproject.com
www.blackcoffeeproject.com

Nishinaka, Jeff
Los Angeles, California
USA
email: paperart@earthlink.net
www.jeffnishinaka.com
www.papercutstudio.net
Bernstein & Andriulli
www.ba-reps.com
phone: (1) 212 682 14 90

Nolte, Anja
Amandastraße 58
20357 Hamburg
Germany
phone: (49) 176 81 07 35 16
email: mail@anjanolte.de
www.anjanolte.de
Margarethe Hubauer - International Illustration

Noper
Romania
email: noper@me.com
www.noper.ro

Norito Miyaki, Alexandre
Rua Av. Cicero Marques, 91 Apt. 32b
82515340 Curitiba
Brazil
phone: (55) 41 92 43 49 48
email: alexandrenorito@gmail.com
www.alexandrenorito.carbonmade.com

O'Brien, James
320 Michigan Street
55102-3106 St. Paul, Minnesota
USA
phone: (1) 651 291 04 26
email: james@obrienart.com
me@jamesobrien.us
www.obrienart.com
www.rappart.com

Okamura, Touko
305,2-30-25, Jingu-mae, Shibuya-ku
150-0001 Tokyo
Japan
phone: (81) 354 74 05 56
fax: (81) 357 86 34 59
email: touko11@mac.com
www.touko.com

Paiva, André
Rua Fiandeiras, 170 conj 41
04545-000, São Paulo
Brazil
phone: (55) 11 37 55 82 00
email: andrepaiva@matosgrey.com.br

Papriko, Ink.
27-18 Idanakano-Cho, Nakahara-Ku
211-0034 Kawasaki-Shi, Kanagawa-Ken
Japan
phone: (81) 90 65 18 08 11
email: mr.papriko@papriko.com
www.papriko.com

Pateman, Paul/Pâté
Coochie Hart
www.coochie-hart.com
phone: (44) 20 77 24 97 00

Patino, Juan
231 NW 85 Place
33126 Miami, Florida
USA
phone: (1) 786 546 8660
email: patinoart@gmail.com
www.juanpablopatino.com

Petridean, Vali
Romania
phone: (40) 743 09 12 34
email: vali@publicis.ro
www.valipetridean.ro

Piglia, Paola
38 St Oswalds Place, Studio 3
SE11 5JE London
United Kingdom
phone: (44) 20 75 87 14 61
fax: (44) 20 75 87 04 16
email: paola@paolapiglia.com
www.paolapiglia.com

PixelPastry
Si Ping, Lim
LASALLE College of the Arts
1 McNally Street
187940 Singapore
Singapore
phone: (65) 6496 52 22
fax: (65) 6496 5111
9 Jalan Tarum
576729 Singapore
Singapore
phone: (65) 92 71 74 02
email: ping@pixel-pastry.com
www.pixel-pastry.com

Potma, Johan
Artbox › centre for creation
Kruislaan 182
1098 SK Amsterdam
The Netherlands
phone: (31) 20 668 15 51
email: info@artbox.nl
www.artbox.nl

Potts, Andy
London
United Kingdom
phone: (44) 20 74 22 83 64
email: info@andy-potts.com
www.andy-potts.com
Anna Goodson Management
www.agoodson.com
phone: (1) 514 482 04 88
Thorogood
www.thorogood.net
(1) 207 691 89 36

Prokopaviciute, Vika
Moscow
Russia
email: prokopaviciute@gmail.com
www.prokopaviciute.com

Puthikulangkura, Surachai
Illusion
62 The Millennia Building, 26th floor(p)
Room no.2601
10330 Luangsuan Road
Lumpini, Bangkok
Thailand
phone: (66) 2 650 50 91
phone: (66) 2 650 50 92
fax: (66) 2 650 50 95
email: Surachai@illusion.co.th
www.illusion.co.th

Rios, Otavio
Faro 22/203 Jardim Botânico
22461-020 Rio de Janeiro
Brazil
phone: (55) 21 99 66 96 15
email: rios.otavio@gmail.com
www.otaviorios.com.br
Bernardo de P.
bernardoromero@uol.com.br

Rodriguez, Edel
16 Ridgewood Ave P.O.BOX 102
07878 Mt. Tabor, New Jersey
USA
phone: (1) 973 983 77 76
email: edelrodriguez@aol.com
www.edelrodriguez.com

Rosen, Kim
7 Kary Street
01060 Northampton, New York
USA
email: kim@kimrosen.com
www.kimrosen.com

Rossi, Alessandro Adelio
Via S. Caterina 55
24124 Bergamo
Italy
phone: (39) 347 36 28 677
email: alessrossi@gmail.com,
info@aarg.it
www.aarg.it

Roth, Chris
538 W. 50th St. 5a
10019 New York
USA
phone: (1) 917 520 75 72
email: chris@chrisroth.net
www.chrisroth.com

Samuels, Graham
Studio Acrobot
Lorensbergsgatan 3b
11733 Stockholm
Sweden
phone: (46) 739 76 59 48
email: mail@grahamsamuels.com
www.grahamsamuels.com
Agent Bauer
www.agentbauer.com

Sassi, Elisa
Av. Giovanni Gronchi 4971 ap 61
5724-003 São Paolo
Brazil
phone: (55) 11 37 42 72 49
email: elissa@gmail.com
www.elisasassi.com

Sawant, Abhishek
Hatiskar Marg
400025 Mumbai
India
phone: (91) 22 24 31 56 25,
phone: (91) 98 67 10 34 57
email: creations.abhishek@gmail.com

Scholten, Cheri
12/3 Tennyson Street, Elwood
VIC 3184
Australia
phone: (61) 401 79 13 16
email: info@verycheri.com,
cheri.scholten@gmail.com
www.verycheri.com

Scott, Edvard
phone: (1) 917 783 21 11
phone: (46) 739 28 50 20
email: me@edvardscott.com
www.edvardscott.com

Scott, Si
55 Britannia Mills, 11 Hulme Hall Rd
M15 4LA Great Manchester
United Kingdom
phone: (44) 78 87 63 79 92
email: si@siscottstudio.com
siscottstudio.com
Levine/Leavitt
www.llreps.com
phone: (1) 212 979 12 00

Seo, Yuhee
20/33-37 Livingstone Road
NSW 2141 Lidcombe
Australia
phone: (61) 449 72 67 24
email: hiyuhee@gmail.com
www.yuheeseo.com

Simpfendoerfer, Thomas
Coherent Images, Digital 3d & Animation
New York
USA
phone: (1) 646 245 5963
email: info@coherentimages.com
www.coherentimages.com
www.ba-reps.com
www.pocko.com

Sköld, Annika
Stora Nygtan 44
111 27 Stockholm
Sweden
phone: (46) 707 22 21 43
email: annika@stockholmillustration.com
www.stockholmillustration.com

sLip
Cincinnati, Ohio
USA
email: sLip@hushmonkeystudios.com

Smith, Dan
The Church Rooms
Agnes Road
NN2 6EU Northampton
United Kingdom
phone: (44) 16 04 45 31 77
fax: (44) 16 04 45 37 43
email: info@enginecreative.co.uk
www.enginecreative.co.uk
Engine Creative Agency Limited
www.enginecreative.co.uk
phone: (44) 16 04 45 31 77

Steblina, Sergey
Chernischevskogo, 94/3a
65017 Odessa
Ukraine
photo: (38) 983 75 89 05
email: sergey@steblina.com
www.steblina.com

Stirling, Caroline
27/159 Union Street Brunswick
3055 Melbourne
Australia
phone: (61) 419 13 96 40
email: contact@carolinestirling.com.au
www.carolinestirling.com.au

Stockton, Frank
120 West Third Street #6
10012 New York
USA
phone: (1) 626 347 9707
email: frank@frankstockton.com
www.frankstockton.com

Stolle, Daniel
Hämeenpuisto 43-45 B 40
33200 Tampere
Finland
phone: (358) 45 232 26 00
email: daniel@d-stolle.de
www.d-stolle.de

Suhariyan, Sonya
Sovetskaya Street,11a
344019 Rostov-on-Don.
Russia
phone: (7) 90 34 01 81 71
email: sonyasuhariyan@gmail.com
www.sonyasuhariyan.com
Illustration Ltd

Székessy, Tanja
Berlin
Germany
phone : (49) 173 459 12 03
email: tanja@szekessy.net
www.szekessy.net
die ILLUSTRATOREN – Corinna Hein
www.illustratoren.de

Tabbutt, Steve
New York
USA
email: stovetabbutt@nyc.rr.com
www.steventabbutt.com
www.morgangaynin.com

Tachimori, Sae
2-8-1 Nishitenma Kita-Ku Osaka
530 0047 Osaka
Japan
phone: (81) 06 63 16 73 63
email: info@visiontrack.jp
aivy-aivy.hp.infoseek.co.jp
vision track
visiontrack.jp

Tan, Chuanda
580 Henry Street, 2
10036 New York
U.S.A.
email: chuanda@mac.com
www.chuandatan.com
www.avemanagement.com

Tavares, Eduardo
Rua 7 de abril, 693 alto da XV
80040-120 Curitiba
Brazil
phone: (55) 41 32 40 14 48
email: tavares@exclam.com.br
www.behance.net/pontodefuga

Taylor, Jay
The Old Hill, Holdiford Road
ST18 0XP Tixall, Stafford
United Kingdom
phone: (44) 78 45 51 73 49
email: JayTaylor@scribblejay.co.uk
www.scribblejay.co.uk

Taylor, Jennifer
835 South Harvey Street
60304 Oak Park, Illinois
USA
phone: (1) 708 948 7195
email: jenn@paperdogstudio.com
www.paperdogstudio.com

Timmins, Mark
London
United Kingdom
phone: (44) 78 70 70 43 26
email: info@marktimmins.co.uk
www.marktimmins.co.uk

Ting, Carson
19 Protea Gardens
M2K 2W5 North York
Canada
phone: (1) 778 991 44 27
email: carson@chairmanting.com
www.chairmanting.com
Denise Cheung
phone: (1) 416 505 89 23
www.chairmanting.com

Troitskaya, Irina
Snezhnaya, 27-2, 297
129323 Moscow
Russia
phone: (7) 499 180 56 09
phone: (7) 905 707 22 51
irina@irtroit.com
www.irtroit.com

Tsaregradskaya, Elena
Bogatyrskiy prospekt, 58/2, appt. 25
197198 Saint Petersburg
Russia
phone: (7) 921 633 61 98
email: info@tsaregradskaya.com
tsaregradskaya.com

Tsou, Page
Flat56 22 Nevern Place
SW5 9PR London
United Kingdom
phone: (44) 77 71 99 54 73
email: chun-sheng.tsou@network.rca.ac.uk
www.pagetsou.com

van den Berg, Eelco
Artbox › centre for creation
Kruislaan 182
1098 SK Amsterdam
The Netherlands
phone: (31) 20 668 15 51
email: info@artbox.nl
www.artbox.nl

Velasco, Johanna V.
35-E Amon Court Salinas Drive, Lahug
6000 Cebu City
Philippines
phone: (63) 916 477 38 31
phone: (63) 32 232 59 24
email: chocolatenostalgia@gmail.com
www.chocolatenostalgia.com

Verhoye, Annabelle Jasmin
26 Bethune Street
10014 New York
USA
phone: (1) 917 685 7550
email: anna@annabelleverhoye.com
www.annabelleverhoye.com

Vidak, Zsolt
Berzenczey u. 37. 5/6
1094 Budapest
Hungary
phone: (36) 20 410 53 57
email: zsolt@vidak.hu
www.vidak.hu

von Bassewitz, David
Kienitzer Str. 108
12049 Berlin
Germany
phone: (49) 30 65 79 96 06
mobile: (49) 160 96 42 57 13
email: mail@davidvonbassewitz.de
www.davidvonbassewitz.net

Wagner, Marco
St.-Brunostr. 10
97204 Höchberg
Germany
phone: (49) 93 14 07 02 34
email: info@marcowagner.net
www.marcowagner.net
Jutta Fricke Illustrators
email: info@jutta-fricke.de

Walker, Neryl
101a Hotham St.
3183 Melbourne
Australia
phone: (61) 430 00 71 37
email: neryl@neryl.com
mail@neryl.com
www.neryl.com

Wearing, Paul
PW Art Limited
41 Carlisle Road
NW6 6TL London
United Kingdom
phone: (44) 20 89 62 69 21
email: paulwearing@illustrator.demon.co.uk
www.paulwearing.co.uk

Weber, Sam
Brooklyn, New York
USA
phone: (1) 917 374 33 73
email: sam@sampaints.com
www.sampaints.com

Webster, Kyle T.
2418 Lyndhurst Ave
27103 Winston-Salem, North Carolina
USA
phone: (1) 336 253 4612
email: kyle@kyletwebster.com

Wiggins, Mick
Berkeley, California
USA
phone: (1) 510 524 3076
email: mick@mickwiggins.com
www.mickwiggins.com

Williams, Jamie
London
United Kingdom
phone: (44) 78 51 56 81 01
email: info@jamiewilliamsartist.com
info@jamiewilliamsartist.com

Wong, Jasper
6781 Hawaii Kai Drive
94107 Honolulu, Hawaii
USA
phone: (1) 510 882 0019
email: sayhi@jasperwong.net
www.jasperwong.net

Wu, Yihsin
No.293-1 Jiaxing Street 1st. floor
11054 Taipei City
Taiwan
email: cocoyi@yahoo.com
www.yihsin.net

Yamada, Yuji
783-4-204 Shibokuchi, Takatsu-ku
213-0023 Kawasaki-shi, Kanagawa
Japan
phone: (81) 44 798 78 67
email: yamada@nh.mods.jp
www.yamada.mods.jp

Zaharova, Alexandra
11, bld. 17, 3 Sokolinoi Gory str.
Moscow
Russia
email: box@paperillustration.ru
www.paperillustration.ru

Ziegler, Julia
Hamburg
Germany
phone: (49) 151 240 77 377
mail: j.ziegler@gmx.net
www.juliaziegler.com

Zoebisch, Alex
Artbox › centre for creation
Kruislaan 182
1098 SK Amsterdam
The Netherlands
phone: (31) 20 668 15 51
email: info@artbox.nl
www.artbox.nl

Illustrator	Country	Category	Page
2FRESH	TUR	Advertising	61
Adolfsson, Mattias	SWE	Books	98
Akane, Showko	JPN	Advertising	55
		Posters	246
Akiyama, Hana	JPN	Advertising	31
Andresen, Meike	GER	Media	231
Araujo, Carlos	BRA	Advertising	32,46
Arocha, Tatiana	USA	Products	182
artbombers	GBR	Advertising	86
Bakal, Scott	USA	Magazine Editorial	161
		Media	224
		Posters	251
Bannecker, Andrew	USA	Advertising	62
		Posters	271
Bates, George	USA	Magazine Editorial	158-159,170-171
Benders, Tessa	NED	Posters	264
Bereciartu, Julia	ESP	Advertising	53
		Cards	124
		Magazine Editorial	161
Bergen, Mats	GER	Magazine Editorial	210
Berning, Tina	GER	Books	114-115
Bertone, Eduardo	ESP	Advertising	72
		Magazine Editorial	201
		Posters	261
Billvik, Lisa	SWE	Magazine Editorial	178
Biyikoglu, Caglar	TUR	Advertising	32,62
		Cards	122,132-133,135
Bolasini, Nicolas	ARG	Books	108
Bonnke, Jens	GER	Magazine Editorial	172
Briers, Stuart	GBR	Advertising	39
Brooks, Jason	GBR	Magazine Editorial	174-177
Brosmind Studio	ESP	Advertising	66-67
Burke, Bernadette	AUS	Advertising	52
Cabadas Reyna, Juan Carlos	MEX	Magazine Editorial	166
Cairanti, Anna	ITA	Books	104
Canetti, Michel	AUS	Advertising	50
Carbone, Noumeda	ITA	Products	277
Carioca	ROM	Advertising	90-91
Carter, Robert	CAN	Magazine Editorial	207
Casassus, Eduardo	CHI	Advertising	64
Chan, Pomme	GBR	Advertising	48
		Magazine Editorial	197
Cheuk, Johnny	HKG	Posters	264
Cohen, Jim	USA	Advertising	54
		CD Design	142
Comforty, Gili	ISR	Media	226-227
Conrad-Hansen, Naja	DEN	Advertising	22
		Posters	255
Cusick, Jonathan	GBR	Magazine Editorial	199
Davis, Brock	USA	Advertising	63
Delorme, Sonia Hidalgo	ESP	Media	229
Despau, David	ESP	Books	99
Deutsch, Mark Joseph	PHI	Advertising	63
Dobric, Danijela	SWE	Advertising	29
		Posters	250
Dociu, Daniel	USA	Media	234-237
Dorn, Erica	GBR	Books	94
Duyker, Marloes	NED	Advertising	20
Eckstrom, Nathaniel	AUS	Magazine Editorial	163
Ellis, Max	GBR	Advertising	72
		Magazine Editorial	206
Elorza, Joseba	ESP	Advertising	27
Falagara, Alexandra	SWE	Magazine Editorial	159
Feindt, Jan	GER	Advertising	79,80
		Calendars	117
		Magazine Editorial	204
		Products	278
Fiedler, Joseph Daniel	USA	Magazine Editorial	212
Flores, Catty	GBR	Books	106
Floship	HGK	Advertising	49
Fluharty, Thomas L.	USA	Magazine Editorial	190
		Posters	269
Franceschini, Matteo	ITA	Posters	260
Fruitós, Adrià	FRA	Books	97
Gabbard, Justin	USA	Advertising	68,69
Galvan, Ana	ESP	Calendars	118-119
		Magazine Editorial	178
Gannenko, Vadim	UKR	Magazine Editorial	200
Garud, Sunil	IND	Advertising	78
Gendron, Cathy	USA	Books	96
		Cards	129
		Magazine Editorial	165
Goddard, Stephane	FRA	Posters	270
Grabarnik, Irina	NED	Posters	243
Grigorev, Alexander	RUS	Cards	135
Guerrero, Karol	ARG	Posters	243
Hajek, Olaf	GER	Advertising	23,24-25
		Magazine Editorial	221
		Posters	265
Hamelink, Coen	DEN	Media	231,238-239
Hancock, James Gulliver	AUS	Covers	145
Harrold, Geoff	GBR	Advertising	26
Hashimoto, Takahisa	JPN	Advertising	17
Haussmann, Martin	GER	Media	225
Headcase Design	USA	Books	109,112-113
		Magazine Editorial	201,202-203, 209
Heatley, David	USA	Magazine Editorial	194
Henao, Andres	USA	CD Design	140
Higasa, Hayato	JPN	Posters	257
Ho, David	USA	CD Design	137
Horvath, Norbert	AUT	Posters	245
Iurissevich, Giulio	ITA	Advertising	53
		Posters	264
Izique, Pedro	BRA	Advertising	56-57,59,81
		Magazine Editorial	184
Jana, Freddy	USA	Advertising	84
		Posters	254
Janus, Agata	POL	Cards	123
Jezierski, Tymek	POL	Magazine Editorial	208
Jome, Hayato	JPN	Cards	134
		Covers	144
Jomepour, Rahele	IRI	Books	102,106
Judge, Chris	IRE	Advertising	71
Kako	BRA	Advertising	37
		Books	116
		Posters	244
Käll, Mattias	SWE	Magazine Editorial	160
IC4DESIGN INC./ Kamigaki, Hirofumi	JPN	Media	232-233
Kaser, Lisa	USA	Cards	122
Kawamoto, Mitsunari	JPN	Advertising	43
		Posters	252
Kinsella III, Edward	USA	Magazine Editorial	185
		Posters	244
Kiskovacs, Eszter	HUN	Advertising	60
Kittozutto	SIN	Advertising	30
Klubnikin, Pavel	UKR	Advertising	84
Knezevic, Aleksandra	BIH	Magazine Editorial	154-155
Kobayashi, Hiromitsu	JPN	Posters	253
Kolesnikov, Ilya	RUS	Products	275
Kolitsch, Petra	GER	Books	107